REDEEMING MODERNITY

D0877910

COMMUNICATION AND HUMAN VALUES

SERIES EDITORS

Robert A. White, Editor, *Centre for the Study of Communication and Culture, London, UK*

Michael Traber, Associate Editor, *World Association for Christian Communication, London, UK*

INTERNATIONAL EDITORIAL ADVISORY BOARD

REDEEMING MODERNITY

MODERNITY
Contradictions in Media Criticism

Joli Jensen

SAGE PUBLICATIONS
The International Professional Publishers
Newbury Park London New Delhi

For information address:

SAGE Publications, Inc.
2455 Teller Road
Newbury Park, California 91320

SAGE Publications Ltd.
6 Bonhill Street
London EC2A 4PU
United Kingdom

SAGE Publications India Pvt. Ltd.
M-32 Market
Greater Kailash I
New Delhi 110 048 India

Printed in the United States of America

Library of Congress Cataloging-in-Publication Data

Jensen, Joli.
   Redeeming modernity : American media criticism as social criticism
/ by Joli Jensen
      p.   cm. — (Communication and human values)
   Includes bibliographical references.
   ISBN 0-8039-3476-9. — ISBN 0-8039-3477-7 (pbk.)
   1. Mass media. 2. Popular culture. 3. Mass media—Social
aspects. 4. Mass media—United States   I. Title. II. Series :
Communication and human values (Newbury Park, Calif.)
P91.J47   1990
302.23'0973—dc20   90-8269
                                                                        CIP

SECOND PRINTING, 1991

Sage Production Editor: Astrid Virding

Contents

Preface   9
Introduction   12
  Structure of the Argument   13
  Participating in the Argument   15
  Limiting the Argument   16

1 Four Critical Voices   18
  Dwight Macdonald: The Media as Mass Culture   20
    The Levels of Modern Culture   22
    Standards of Evaluation   23
    The Tepid Ooze of Midcult   24
    The Cultivation of Audiences   25
    The Problem of Democratic Culture   26
  Daniel Boorstin: The Media as Spectacular Illusion 30
    The Pseudo-Event   30
    Extravagant Expectations   31
    The Graphic Revolution   32
    The Thicket of Unreality   32
    Dissolving Forms   34
    The Menace of Unreality   35
  Stuart Ewen: The Media as Ideological Apparatus   38
    Captains of Industry/Captains of Consciousness   39
    Defining the Social Realm   41
    Commercializing Expression   41
    Control of the Social Realm   41
  Neil Postman: The Media as Corrosive Amusement   44
  Macdonald, Boorstin, Ewen, Postman: What the Media Do   50
    Media as Transformative Power   52
    The Public as Media Victims   53

2 Media in Modernity   57
     The Possibility of Progress   58
     The Modernity Story   59
     The Duality of Modernity   63
     The Modern as Mass Society   65
     American Modernity   71
          Community/Society   71
          Authority/Power   74
          Class/Status   78
          Sacred/Secular   80
          Alienation/Progress   83
     Media/Modernity as Inauthentic Other   85
     Polluting the Future   88
     The World of Tomorrow   90
     Media as New Technologies   94
     Media as Technological Progress   96

3 Three Dominant Metaphors   101
     The Media as Art   103
          Timeless and Transcendent Truth   105
          Cultural Levels   111
          Aesthetic Communities   113
          The Myth of the Artist   115
          American Faultlines   116
          The Problem of Democratic Art   117
          The Problem of Democratic Taste   121
          Summary   123
     The Media as Information   124
          Theoretical Underpinnings   127
          News as Modern Information   129
          Theories of an American Press   133
          Lippmann and Dewey   137
          Information in Entertainment   140

The Media as Education   145
   Commercial Education via the Media   147
   Vulnerable Children   150
   Hypnotic Media Power   150
   Theories of Media Influence   151
   Summary   154
  Conclusions   156

4 Characteristics of Media Discourse   159
  Essential Worth   161
  Lowest Common Denominator?   163
  Egalitarian Elitism   164
  The Contamination Theme   166
  Blurring Boundaries   167
  The Pure and the Polluting   168
   Reason/Emotion   168
   Art/Commerce   170
  Media Minglings   171
  Corruption and Deflection   174

5 Recognitions and Reconceptualizations   177
  Media Power   180
  Redemptive Forms   183
  Historical Trajectories   191
  Immanence as Transcendence   194
  Consequences of Reconceptualization   196
  Recognizing the Dream   199

References   202
Index   207
About the Author   221

Preface

The impetus for this book was a seminar on media, culture, and society, held at the University of Virginia in 1985. Faculty members from a variety of disciplines gathered to consider the role of mass communication in modern life. Four media scholars—James Carey, Michael Schudson, Horace Newcomb, and John Pauly—each of whom had significantly shaped my thinking, were featured speakers. Their presentations were wonderful—subtle, thoughtful, and intellectually rich. Yet the discussions that followed were frustratingly narrow and repetitive. Renowned scholars in history, literature, philosophy, and sociology seemed unable to shed their mistrust of, and disdain for, mass communication in any form. They returned over and over to a monolithic vision of the mass media as individual, social, and cultural corruption. As I struggled to understand why they would not, or could not, get past this vision to engage the complexities of the presentations, this book began to form.

The seminar demonstrated to me the existence of a coherent climate of opinion about media-in-society, a climate that informs scholarly accounts as well as popular commentary, casual conversations, and daily experiences. This climate dominates discussions of how the media figure in contemporary life. By examining here the explicit and implicit logic operating in claims of media influence, I have sought to analyze this climate so that we can recognize and surpass it.

This analysis has grown out of my teaching, which began, interestingly enough, by elaborating on the claims I now critique. When I first started teaching courses in media, culture, and society, I did so believing that the media (at least the current electronic media) embodied the corruptions of modern life. I gathered the articles that argue that modern life is increasingly alienating, that modern culture is increasingly trivial, that modern experience is increasingly unsatisfying, and that modern knowledge is increasingly shallow. By using these scholasticized accounts of familiar arguments, it was easy to demonstrate to students that their ambivalence about mass media existed because the media deepen and extend the corrosive characteristics of modernity.

After a semester of reading discussions of the role of media in modern life, we had erudite justification for believing that we (or at least the nebulous "everybody else") were victims of media manipulation and modernity's confines. We were trapped at an unhappy moment in history, cut off from the possibilities of the past and blocked from the promise of the future. The mass media were deeply implicated in our impasse.

This claustrophobic conclusion offers little solace. The readings, and our discussions of them, left us with only a feeble, individual antidote—critical wariness. All I could offer my students (and myself) were exhortations to be alert to the dangerous influences that surround us, in the hope that this knowledge would mitigate the influences of media in modernity. This is the dispiriting end-point of the dominant media critique—a call for increased critical capacity, so that at least some of us will not fully succumb.

I still teach this apocalyptic vision of seductive media, a vulnerable audience, and the corruption of social possibility, because it still suffuses discussions of the role of media-in-society. But I no longer believe it. Now I seek to explain why it prevails, and why it is so convincing. My goal has become to figure out, with my students, why contemporary cultural forms and practices are so mistrusted and so readily vilified.

This attempt to understand, and then rethink, the prevailing climate of opinion forces us to reexamine fundamental beliefs. It becomes an exercise in examining how and why we think in the ways that we do. In my classes, we locate patterns of belief and see how the same kinds of arguments have been made about different media over time. We recognize the ways in which the same terms, concepts, and stories recur, and this helps us move beyond a repetitive blaming of the media and into discussion of the fundamental assumptions upon which such blame is based. This discussion makes possible the consideration of alternative ways to conceptualize the role of mass communication in society.

I hope that this discussion, and subsequent consideration of alternatives, becomes available to you in the pages that follow. Friends, teachers, and colleagues have encouraged me during these years of rethinking the taken-for-granted; I can mention only a few of them here. First are my teachers at the Institute of Communications Research, particularly Jim Carey, whose work first drew me into the field and whose example continues to sustain me. Next are my former colleagues in the Department of Rhetoric and Communication Studies at the University of Virginia, particularly Bill Miller, who encouraged an early version of this book, and John Rodden, who accompanied its beginnings and completion. Finally, there are my colleagues in the Radio-Television-Film Department at the University of Texas—Austin, particularly Horace Newcomb, who read through two very different drafts with characteristic insight. Enthusiastic commentary on an early version by John Pauly, now at the University of Tulsa, kept me going.

My editor, Bob White, now at the Gregorian University in Rome, helped me turn a series of ambitious and elliptical essays into a sustained, and (I hope) accessible argument. His willingness to get inside the ideas and offer careful reading and response represents the ideal editorial guidance.

Finally, I want to acknowledge the fundamental influence of my students in Illinois, Virginia, and Texas, each of whom has helped me recognize and develop the ideas that follow. I am always grateful for their energy, skepticism, and encouragement.

—*Joli Jensen*
Austin, Texas

Introduction

There is a deep ambivalence in our attitudes toward the mass media. As we watch television, go to movies, listen to the radio, attend to the news, we feel uneasy about something called "the media," and uncomfortable with "its" possible influence on us and others. While we may make exceptions for certain kinds of content, we tend to assume that the overall influence of the mass media on society is dangerous, and therefore we distrust the role of the media in our lives.

As members of contemporary society, we are aware of a general climate of opinion about media influence. We know that the media, so widespread, ubiquitous, and appealing, have been accused of misleading individuals, misrepresenting reality, commercializing feelings, and, in general, corrupting contemporary life. Our ambivalence about our own participation in popular forms of communication stems from the demonic image that dominates discussions of the role of mass communication in society—an image of the media as a monolithic, and malevolent, force.

This book seeks to explain how and why such an image has been sustained in American thought. I believe that the prevailing conceptualizations of media-in-society truncate our ability to teach, write, and talk about this central component of our common life. Because of this, I have sought ways to clarify the connections I see, in media discourse, between beliefs about the mass media and beliefs about modernity. I demonstrate how the mass media operate as scapegoats for a deeper ambivalence about modern life. I describe an underlying narrative of seduction and betrayal that orients the discourse on media-in-society and locate contradictory metaphors that structure it. I argue that media criticism proceeds in the ways that it does because it offers commentators (and therefore us) a way to avoid a direct confrontation with persistent contradictions in American social thought.

The Structure of the Argument

Why are the mass media so readily cast as evil outsiders that wreak havoc on vulnerable people, ride roughshod over fragile cultural traditions, and represent the bane of contemporary life? The most obvious answer is "Because it's true." Yet media commentary proceeds, convincingly, at solely a narrative level. Media commentary can be understood as a more general discourse that mobilizes and reproduces assumptions about history, culture, society, and technology. *Discourse* refers to an intersecting set of self-validating beliefs about what was, what now is, and what ought to be. Thus the media discourse operates as a coherent social narrative, one that does not, and need not, rely on outside evidence to be convincing.

As such, it takes on the characteristics of myth, legend, and folktale. Disturbing "evidence" of media influence—addicted children, deranged fans, copycat killers—mingles with more evanescent claims about the commercialization of art and politics and the fragmenting of contemporary consciousness. The coherent narrative of media-in-society is elaborately woven from fragile but frightening threads, and the result is an almost impenetrable climate of opinion about the "badness" of the media.

Social narratives are convincing because they engage and confirm taken-for-granted assumptions about the world. This means that they are particularly hard to analyze, refute, or surpass. But if we can temporarily suspend our belief in a particular social narrative and examine its central terms and logic, we can at least partially question its usefulness. At the very least, such a suspension and examination can tell us much about the values we hold dear and the beliefs we use to understand and evaluate our common experience. Thus media commentary, as a discourse, can become a lens through which to explore an implicit, often unrecognized, terrain of social and cultural beliefs. Once we have "seen" this terrain through this lens, we can suggest different ways to think, believe, and evaluate.

The central subject of this book is the terrain of values and beliefs that are mobilized in commentaries on the role of media-in-society. My goal is to locate and clarify the fundamental assumptions that operate in this terrain, in order to make them available for reassessment. Such a reassessment can foster, I believe, more fruitful and illuminating ways to think about mass communication in modern life.

I focus this analysis on American commentary, although the characteristics of American discourse have come to dominate international considerations of media influence. American media criticism proceeds in relation to ideas, values, and beliefs about the possibilities of modernity, and the relationship between media and modernity is of global concern. Yet my interest here is in uncovering how media discourse connects up with particularly American historical, cultural, and social expectations; much work remains to be done on how other nations construct and sustain comparable narratives.

I begin with a close analysis of arguments by four well-known American critics. The nature of their critiques is described to illustrate exactly how something called "the media" can be deemed to cause individual, cultural, and social harm. Their claims become a common foundation for later examination of the general terrain of American media discourse.

These four specific critiques, and their particular claims, are then temporarily bracketed in order to explore their larger context—the conceptualization of modernity. Claims about media influence are most fully understood, I will show, in relation to congruent claims about the nature of the past, the characteristics of the present, and the possibilities of the future.

In this way, media criticism is shown to intersect with social criticism—the two represent different aspects of a more general discourse on modernity.

The heart of the book is where the characteristics and contradictions of media discourse are foregrounded, historically located, and made available for rethinking. The social narrative of media influence is described in relation to particular strategies and metaphors. The evaluation of media in relation to ideal forms of art, information, education, and technology, grounded in a myth of seduction and betrayal, is described.

The consequences of the dominant media discourse are in relation to what it obscures and what it implies. Throughout my analysis I address the contradictions that are hidden by the ways we tell the story of media influence. In the concluding chapter I discuss these contradictions directly, and consider why they are obscured in the discourse. The ways we think about media-in-society allow us to blame the media as an outside influence that deflects or deforms social progress. Thus the dominant media discourse constructs a self-serving account, one that allows us to blame the media for the loss of an imagined past or desirable future, and keeps us from confronting the character of, and contradictions in, all social change.

Participating in the Argument

This analysis of the characteristics of media discourse requires a special kind of engagement on the part of the reader. I am asking that you acknowledge and reexamine your assumptions about media influence, and about modern life. This is not easy, because these assumptions are the "givens" in everyday conversation, popular commentary, and scholarly essays. I am asking you, the reader, to reexamine your own presuppositions in relation to the assumptions that I locate, describe, and critique. I, as author, am interpreting interpretations; you are being asked to interpret my interpretations of the interpretations, in the light of your own assumptions and beliefs.

This can be a frustrating experience, because there is no solid ground on which to stand. My analysis of interpretations proceeds without the reassuring presence of "hard facts" (beyond the arguments of critics who are interpreting the "facts") or "hard theory" (beyond the structures of assumptions I locate in others' works, and bring to bear in my own analyses). You are being asked to follow along with my reading of someone else's reading of media effects or modernity's influence, while at the same time putting your own sense of media and modernity at risk.

Limiting the Argument

Some disclaimers need to be made. I am not seeking to prove or disprove actual media effects on society. Given the nature of the relationships among media, technology, culture, and society, and the scope of current modes of inquiry, I am not convinced that incontrovertible proof can be gathered, or that it should be sought. Here I am simply assuming that the most demonstrable aspect of media-in-society is the commentary it has sparked. I take the history of *discussion* of the influence of media on modern life to be more interesting and important than available analyses of "actual" media effects.

This is not to say that I necessarily celebrate or applaud whatever roles the mass media may play in contemporary life. It would be easy to misconstrue my analysis of media discourse as, by inference, a flimsy celebration of the status quo. Media commentary is inevitably cultural and social evaluation, and thus it is always political. No one can or should enter this terrain in neutral. I share with many of the critics of media and modern life concerns about how to achieve and protect social justice, cultural richness, and individual freedoms. What I seek here is a clarification, and a refiguring, of the ways in which to imagine and realize these goals.

It would be possible, too, to misconstrue my argument as a cavalier dismissal of the long history of media effects research. In this work I am not claiming that no media effects have ever been demonstrated, only that these demonstrations do not connect up with the dominant discourse on media influence. Whatever the merits of the communication effects research, commentators rarely draw on it to bolster their claims, and, even when they do, it is usually through a misreading, or a misapplication, of findings. The logic of media discourse is that the influence of the mass media on individuals and society is intuitively obvious—it needs merely to be exposed, then condemned.

Finally, I am not claiming to offer a summary of all the claims ever made about media influence, in order to pave the way for their replacement by a single "correct" view. I am not dismissing all former claims as "wrong" in order to offer claims of my own triumphantly as "right." I am instead trying to pave the way for us to think more deeply, carefully, and richly about the complex role of media in modern life.

This can be achieved, I believe, by first locating the terms in which we think. Until we become aware of the terms, categories, and presuppositions with which we think, we cannot get past them into other, more illuminating ones. I believe that we have been "thinking with" certain media metaphors for so long that they are taken for true, and that this prevents us from thinking usefully about the ways that mass communication and modernity intersect.

Once the connections between the media and modernity critiques are clarified, both can be directly addressed. We can find better terms for our common discussion of media-in-society if we can recognize the tenacity, and inadequacies, of the ways we now tell the story of media influence. We need to find ways to get past the narrative that now dominates popular discussion, a narrative that blames the media for what has gone wrong (and should have gone right) in modernity.

1

Four Critical Voices

Media discourse offers us a circumscribed body of literature that makes assumptions about our common life. It can tell us what we are telling ourselves about the past, present, and future, about what has happened, what holds true now, and what will come to pass. But before this body of commentary can be made to speak in this way, it must be unpacked and analyzed. This process becomes, then, a critique of the critique.

Such unpacking and analysis is no easy task. The development of commercial forms of mass communication (including the book, the newspaper, telegraphy, photography, film, and broadcasting) has been accompanied by a cacophony of commentary. Numerous writers have made, and continue to make, numerous claims about the implications of mass communication. The media have been attacked by radicals, conservatives, and liberals, by those who work in the media and by those to whom they are addressed, by elitists and by populists, by teachers, preachers, politicians, and journalists, in the name of such values as art, truth, morality, democracy, knowledge, experience, and "the people."[1] Each critic marshals a flexible array of ammunition, drawn from a storehouse of values that is always in flux. In short, the media critique is not simple or unitary, nor has it remained historically the same.

Yet, if we are to interrogate media criticism for what it can reveal about the terms in which we think about our common life, then we must find ways to examine, carefully and fairly, the nature of the claims being made. We must, temporarily at least, look beneath the claims to recognize the implicit assumptions on which they rest, seeking general patterns, or consistent elements, or recurring contradictions.

There have been several attempts to organize the body of commentary on media-in-society.[2] These valuable efforts leave a daunting list of charges or assumptions at the doorstep of the mass media. What such lists offer us is a way to freeze, combine, and then respond to the most common claims about media influence—they tell us what the claims are. What they cannot tell us, because they do not historically ground or contextualize the commentary, is *why* the media are critiqued in the ways that they are.

Further, in media discourse, the object of criticism is always slippery. When something called The Media is invoked, the critic may mean media content (what is in movies or on television or on the radio or in the newspaper) or specific media forms (advertising or entertainment or news) or particular technologies (electronic versus cinematic versus print versus oral forms of communication) or modern cultural processes in general (widely available, commercially produced and distributed symbolic material). A critic can use some fluctuating combination of these referents in discussion, moving from comments on content to form to technology to general culture without specifying what aspect of The Media is being discussed.

To clarify not only what is being criticized, but in which terms and for what purposes, it is useful to begin this analysis with specific critics. My goal is, first, to uncover coherent individual arguments, based on implicit and explicit assumptions about media influence in relation to society, economics, politics, culture, and history.

I begin by summarizing four widely read books, all of which deal with media influence: *Against the American Grain*, by Dwight Macdonald (1962); *The Image*, by Daniel Boorstin (1972); *Captains of Consciousness*, by Stuart Ewen (1976); and *Amusing Ourselves to Death* by Neil Postman (1985).[3] None of the authors of these books is exclusively a media critic—each has written books on other matters, and each examines from a different intellectual tradition: Macdonald from literary criticism, Boorstin from history, Ewen from economics and sociology, and Postman from education and communications.

Each book makes a distinctive argument, and can be seen as representing different dominant threads in media criticism as a whole. Finally, while the original publication of each book can seem to offer a critical trajectory from the spread of television in the 1950s,[4] such a tracing would be suspect, since each critic builds his own case, with little overt reliance on previous or concurrent claims about media influence.

I discuss each book as fairly as I can, in its own terms. This offers a common ground on which to begin an examination of the fundamental characteristics of media criticism. When there are obvious commonalities or differences among these four authors, I point them out, but the dominant aim in this first chapter is descriptive analysis—laying out and making accessible the general claims of four particular critics of media influence. In a later section I will explore the fundamental metaphors these authors share with other critics, and draw out the narrative strategies on which these metaphors rely.

Dwight Macdonald:
The Media as Mass Culture

Media criticism in the 1950s and early 1960s was dominated by concern with what was called "mass culture." The central issues, at least among cultural critics, were the influences of the mass media on art and on what was termed "folk culture." Critics considered, as well, the influence of mass culture on the aesthetic capabilities of the media audience.

The "mass culture debate," waged mostly in essays by literary and social critics, addressed the general fate of culture in modern society. As such, the debate still includes intractable issues in the relationship among media, culture, and society. The aim of the debate, in its earliest essays, was to define the differences among mass culture, folk culture, and high culture, and then to discuss what needed to be done to protect and promote the "best" forms of culture.

In the mass culture debate, the mass media are represented as purveyors of corrupt and corrupting cultural forms. They are seen, basically, as vehicles of debased content, vehicles that are becoming increasingly popular and ubiquitous. The mass media are also seen as "culture industries," conglomerations of bureaucratized culture production that crank out a never-ending flow of mediocre cultural content.

The connecting thread in Dwight Macdonald's (1962) essay collection *Against the American Grain* is his concern with the influence of mass culture on high culture. He writes from a position of guarded pessimism—his claim is that mass culture is an inescapable aspect of modern industrial life, and that high culture is in most danger not from it, but from a corrupt hybrid, which he dubs Midcult.

Macdonald remains best remembered, and is still cited, for his descriptions of three levels of modern culture (Masscult, Midcult, and High Culture) and his memorable dispatching of beloved (but Midcult) cultural forms like Wilder's *Our Town*, Norman Rockwell paintings, *Life* magazine, and the Book-of-the-Month Club. But Macdonald's essay "Masscult & Midcult," when read in the context of *Against the American Grain* and in relation to its earlier versions, consciously and even painfully develops many of the key ambivalences that still figure in American cultural criticism. When an American cultural critic confronts mass media content, he or she must also confront an American heritage of egalitarian populism—Macdonald is acutely aware of the antidemocratic implications of making value hierarchies for cultural material, and of condemning popular taste.

So Macdonald does not simply or easily construct absolute cultural levels, nor does he cavalierly relegate various cultural products to various cultural strata. Yet he does, ultimately, make a strong case for maintaining distinctions among cultural levels, and for the need to defend high culture against the

homogenizing, diluting, debasing forces of Masscult and Midcult. Because he makes this case while recognizing and responding to charges of elitism and undemocratic snobbishness,
he offers us a way to examine important claims and contradictions in American cultural critiques of the mass media.

The Levels of Modern Culture

The key to Macdonald's argument is his positing of a historically new cultural form—mass culture. He calls it Masscult
(because it does not deserve the term *culture*) and connects its
development with the Industrial Revolution and the concomitant rise of a new, amorphous, semiliterate, semieducated middle class. Before the end of the eighteenth century, Macdonald
argues, "the people" played little role in history or in culture;
after the eighteenth century, they became a cultural market, and
thus a cultural force.

For Macdonald, mass culture is a specious transformation of
Folk Art, the culture it displaces. Folk Art comes from "below,"
it was "the people's own institution, their private little kitchen-
garden walled off from the great formal park of their masters"
(p. 14). Mass culture, on the other hand, comes from "above,"
and is "fabricated by technicians hired by business men." In
Masscult, "everything becomes a commodity, to be mined for
$$$$" (p. 27), it is "not just unsuccessful art. It is non-art. It is
even anti-art."

Art, or High Culture, is not, for Macdonald, some absolute
canon of "greats." He believes that most High Culture has been
"undistinguished, since talent is always rare—one has only to
walk through any great art museum or try to read some of the
forgotten books from the past century . . . there were really just
a few plums in a pudding of mediocrity" (p. 4). Yet High
Culture, "however inept, is an expression of feelings, ideas,
tastes, visions that are idiosyncratic and the audience similarly
responds to them as individuals" (p. 5). In contrast,

Masscult offers its customers neither an emotional catharsis nor an
aesthetic experience, for these demand effort. The production line

grinds out a uniform product whose humble aim is not even entertainment, for this too implies life and hence effort, but merely
distraction. It may be stimulating or narcotic, but it must be easy to
assimilate. It asks nothing of its audience, for it is "totally subjected
to the spectator" [Malraux]. And it gives nothing. (pp. 4-5)

We can infer, from this, some of the characteristics that define
High Culture for Macdonald—High Culture is idiosyncratic
expression that is individual in its creation and reception; it
allows members of the audience to experience emotional catharsis, or to have "an aesthetic experience"; such an experience
is demanding of the audience, and offers us "something." In
contrast, Masscult is formulaic, "ground out" on a production
line, in order to distract us. It asks nothing and offers nothing—
it is banal tripe, commercially produced by technicians for an
amorphous mass public.

Already a series of metaphors and assumptions have been
put into play. A contrast is implied between the "individual"
and the "mass" mind, between aesthetic experience and distraction, between demanding and undemanding content, between
individual and industrial modes of production. These characteristics distinguish the levels of culture and can be determined,
apparently, from the critic's own responses to the particular
material.

Standards of Evaluation

The key distinction between Masscult and High Culture is,
for Macdonald, the notion of standards within a community of
creators and audience. He returns frequently to the issue of
standards in his essays, but in relation to shared, communal
standards, rather than absolute ones. It is the intimacy, the
shared sensibility of the intellectual/artistic community that
ultimately allows High Culture to flourish.

If creators and audience share sensibilities, then the cultural
form is worthy. This is the case in Folk Art, as well as in High
Culture. With the Industrial Revolution and the new, loose,
abstract social relations of mass society, he argues, this commu-

nity of shared standards is impossible. When, as in Masscult and Midcult, creators pander to or exploit their audiences with marketable plots and formulae, then the cultural form is unworthy. When the only standard that matters is how popular a cultural item is, there are no real standards except marketability.

The Tepid Ooze of Midcult

It is Midcult, however, that most infuriates Macdonald because it displays the noxious elements of Masscult while pretending to represent the standards of High Culture.

> The danger to High Culture is not so much from Masscult as from a peculiar hybrid bred from the latter's unnatural intercourse with the former. A whole middle culture has come into existence and it threatens to absorb both its parents. This intermediate form—let us call it Midcult—has the essential qualities of Masscult—the formula, the built-in reaction, the lack of any standard except popularity—but it decently covers them with a cultural figleaf. In Masscult the trick is plain—to please the crowd by any means. But Midcult has it both ways: it pretends to respect the standards of High Culture while in fact it waters them down and vulgarizes them. (p. 37)

Midcult is a corruption of High Culture, hollow and pretentious. It incorporates the avant-garde, thus appearing to be advanced and sophisticated, but in actuality it is produced by "lapsed avant-gardists who know how to use the modern idiom in the service of the banal" (p. 51). Midcult is dangerous because it masquerades as the real thing, and thus it is taken to be the real thing by audiences.

In positing Midcult as the real danger to High Culture, Macdonald uses images of guerrilla warfare. Because High Culture can easily be distinguished from Masscult, it remains protected—recognizable and defensible. Midcult, however, sneaks over the barricades because it resembles, is taken to be, is treated as, High Culture.

Disguised in avant-garde trappings and laden with critical acclaim and prestigious awards, these derivative, banal, trite, and facile Midcult forms will take the fort. The danger is that no one will be able to tell the ersatz from the real—the fear is that the values of Midcult will "now themselves become a debased, permanent standard" (p. 55).

The Cultivation of Audiences

Like many cultural critics, Macdonald implicitly uses a metaphor of cultivation—we become what we are surrounded by—in combination with a metaphor of ingestion—we become what we consume. If we are surrounded by a tepid ooze of Midcult, we lose our ability to discriminate between the derivative and the original. If we are enveloped in Masscult, we grow accustomed to being exploited, talked down to, degraded.

This happens to both the audiences and the creators of cultural objects. "Those who consume Masscult might as well be eating ice-cream sodas, while those who fabricate it are no more expressing themselves than are the 'stylists' who design the latest atrocity from Detroit" (p. 5). The masses have been "debauched" by their exposure to Masscult and Midcult and, after several generations, have come to "demand such trivial and comfortable cultural products" (p. 72).

This sounds, then, as if the masses could potentially be redeemed or restored if they were exposed to High Culture in unadulterated form. This was, in fact, Macdonald's original position—in his 1944 version of the essay ("A Theory of Popular Culture") he called for the integration of the masses into High Culture. But, he reports in the preface to *Against the American Grain*, he later lost faith in that possibility, and believes now that there need to be two separate and distinct cultural classes—elite high culture and general mass culture:

> So let the masses have their Masscult, let the few who care about good writing, painting, music, architecture, philosophy etc., have their High Culture, and don't fuzz up the distinction with Midcult. (p. 73)

The Problem of Democratic Culture

This separatist solution to the deleterious influence of media-distributed Masscult and Midcult is, Macdonald claims, a compromise position between conservative and liberal approaches to the mass culture problem. It neither reinstates a traditional elite based on class distinctions (ostensibly the conservative position) nor attempts to uplift the level of Masscult and Midcult and thus the masses who consume them (supposedly the liberal position).

Further, he claims, it views the masses neither as automatically cheap and vulgar (he ascribes this view to the conservatives) nor as the unwitting dupes of cultural exploitation (a view he ascribes to liberal sociologists and "Marxian radicals"). Rather, it recognizes the inescapability of a "reciprocating engine" of culture/society, where the production of debased culture stimulates a demand for it, which stimulates its production. This chicken-egg process, according to Macdonald, "shows no signs of running down" (p. 72).

And yet, Macdonald himself brings up, sometimes gingerly, even coyly, the problem of defining and defending aesthetic hierarchies in a democratic society. In a telling footnote, he discusses an attack on his views after his presentation in London at a *New Left Review* forum. After his talk criticizing American mass culture, he reports that he was surprised to find British students defending Hollywood (in the name of democracy) as a genuine, valuable expression of mass taste. He writes:

> They seemed to think it snobbish of me to criticize our movies and television from a serious viewpoint. Since I had been criticizing Hollywood for some thirty years, and always with the good conscience one has when one is attacking from the Left, this proletarian defense of our peculiar institution left me rather dazed. (pp. 64-65)

But he was not so dazed as to miss the key differences between his perspective and theirs—he clearly delineates the crucial distinctions. He writes that *he* sees cultural lines as "dikes against corruption," whereas the British students saw them as "relics of a snobbish past." He sees standards as defining, they saw them as inhibiting. He sees tradition as nourishing, they saw it as deadening.

In this footnote Macdonald neatly lays out some of the fundamental contradictions inherent in an American critique of popular culture. He also presages the crucial differences among combatants in current debates about the core curriculum in American universities. Current cultural criticism, especially as influenced by poststructuralism, neo-Marxism, and feminism, must struggle with how to think about lines of demarcation, standards, and tradition. Do standards liberate or oppress? In whose interests are cultural demarcations drawn? Does tradition enrich or stultify?

These questions are peculiarly poignant in American cultural thought. Given the liberal American faith in the possibilities of popular rule, based in a throwing off of the bonds of class, status, history, and tradition, it is always awkward for an American critic to defend beliefs in cultural and social distinctions, evaluative standards, the vital role of history and tradition. It is particularly discomfiting when one attempts to do so in the name of "the people," when "the people" continually embrace the very cultural forms the critics most despise.

I discuss in a later section how the question of what constitutes a worthy democratic culture has haunted American social critics. Here it is important to note that Macdonald's two-culture "compromise" is an uneven, but characteristically American, attempt to support the possibility of participatory, pluralistic American culture, while arguing for the existence of elite sensibilities that require protection from the taint of popular cultural forms.

Macdonald stops short of blaming the masses (the "reciprocating engine") but also of respecting their choices (which he characterizes as debauched, deformed, banal); he criticizes the culture industries, but not in relation to capitalism; he criticizes "the system" but does not call for any real change in it. Instead, in a very American way, he calls for a kind of "freedom of choice"—to each his or her own chosen cultural level. His major suggestion is the development of a kind of esprit de corps among (quoting Stendhal) "we happy few" who care about good culture. He seeks the development of a public consciousness "insisting on higher standards and setting itself off—joyously, implacably—from most of its fellow citizens, not only from the Masscult depths but also from the agreeable ooze of the Midcult swamp" (p. 74).

This elides, rather than resolves, the many contradictions of the American mass culture critique. Macdonald eloquently sidesteps a number of issues other critics also tap dance around. These issues center on the notion of intrinsic aesthetic qualities, absolute aesthetic standards, the nature of popularization, the relationship between text and audience, the categorization of culture, and the blurring of distinctions.

Can cultural forms be evaluated by absolute aesthetic standards? To say yes is to assume that there are "given" qualities, reliably located in cultural objects, that inevitably make some forms of culture more worthy than others. But these assumptions are being questioned by those who note how the cultural forms of the privileged are always valued as better than those of the marginalized. It is increasingly recognized that aesthetic standards are established, not given, are ascribed, not inherent, and that they inevitably reproduce existing status hierarchies.

Does popularization inevitably vulgarize? To say yes is to assume that whatever is widely accessible and appreciated is automatically less worthy than that which is obscure and even disliked by "the masses." This is an antipopulist stance that is not easy to sustain in American thought.

Does culture *cultivate* an audience—do we become what we "consume"? The relationship between text and audience is a complex one, and media commentary relies on a cultivation metaphor. It is assumed that we, the audience, somehow absorb the goodness and subtlety of worthy culture, thus becoming uplifted and refined ourselves. Similarly, we absorb the corruption or triviality of symbolic expression, becoming corrupt or trivial ourselves. Thus cultural forms are given the power to make us over in their (assumed) image.

Does culture indeed come in watertight compartments, as Macdonald argues, and does a blurring of distinctions automatically result in a reduction of quality? The creation and maintenance of cultural boundaries is a crucial issue in media commentary, and we will see how demarcation relies on an assumed distinction between the pure and the corrupt. This distinction deserves interrogation—if cultural standards are ascribed, not given, then the maintenance of categorical distinctions supports hierarchies that anoint the elite few and repudiate the popular many. Again, this is a discomfiting possibility in American life, where notions of an inclusive, egalitarian culture remain tenacious.

Macdonald is sensitive to the complex connections between culture and society, and to the implications of his evaluative scheme. He sees mass culture as intrinsically related to the rise of mass society, and is careful to point out that "the masses" are neither as passive and exploited as (he says) the Left claims nor as barbarous and dangerous as (he says) the Right implies. They are instead, he argues, an aggregation of individuals in modern social relationships, bereft of the communal relations that nurture and sustain aesthetic quality.

Macdonald seeks, finally, circumscribed cultural activity, with the media as purveyors of Masscult for the masses who have been cultivated to enjoy it, and the intellectual weeklies as purveyors of High Culture for the "happy few" who are able to know and appreciate it. Macdonald does not explain how the "happy few" come into existence nor how—unlike the masses—only their particular lives are enriched and ennobled by their cultural alliances. Beneath the surface of Macdonald's "literary analysis" are aesthetic, social, political, economic, and cultural questions of stunning complexity, questions that the mass culture debate can raise but not resolve.

We will see (in Chapter 3) how Macdonald's point of view connects with a more general critical perspective, one that evaluates the mass media as an art form and invokes an American heritage of assumptions about the redemptive possibilities of democratic art. For now, we turn from Macdonald's analysis of the media as mass culture to Boorstin's analysis of the media as illusory images, as we continue to use individual critics to develop an exemplary terrain of concerns about the influence of media on American society.

Daniel Boorstin:
The Media as Spectacular Illusion

While there is some overlap between Macdonald's concerns and Boorstin's, Boorstin's argument rest on a very different metaphor. Media content is not primarily aesthetic for Boorstin, and his concern is not with the fate of High Culture or Folk Art. He does not discuss the concomitant emergence of mass society and mass culture, nor is he particularly interested in the state of democratic art in contemporary America.

Boorstin's concern is with truth, not culture—with actuality, not art. What Boorstin (1972) addresses in *The Image: A Guide to Pseudo-Events in America* is how the mass media deceive us by offering us illusions, illusions that come increasingly to substitute for genuine experience. His dominant metaphor is one of vision—how can we see the world aright when we live in a mediated fog of "bewitching unrealities"?

The Pseudo-Event

The key concept in *The Image*, and the one that is most often attached to Boorstin's name, is that of the pseudo-event. Boorstin distinguishes between the "synthetic novelty" of pseudo-events staged, planned, planted, or incited in order to be reported or disseminated (such as grand openings of new stores, anniversaries of events, interviews, press releases, political debates) and "actual reality," which he claims is spontaneous, unplanned, natural. "There remains," he says, "a tantalizing difference between man-made and God-made events" (p. 11).

Boorstin believes that pseudo-events have become our contemporary reality. He argues that pseudo-events are, by their nature, more interesting and attractive to us than unmediated reality. Pseudo-events are particularly suited to news processes, because they are intrinsically more dramatic than naturally occurring events, easier to disseminate, endlessly repeatable, easily intelligible, and, therefore, ultimately reassuring.

Thus, for Boorstin, pseudo-events have become journalism, and vice versa. "More and more," he says, "news events become dramatic performance" (p. 16) and journalists become, not reporters of real occurrences, but, instead, "dramatic critics." Freedom of the press, which was "once an institution preserved in the interest of the community" is now "a euphemism for the prerogative of reporters to produce their synthetic commodity" (p. 29).

Knowledge of pseudo-events comes to represent useful knowledge of "the world"; the "well-informed citizen" is informed mostly by pseudo-events defined as news. Most frightening to Boorstin is that, with the proliferation of pseudo-events, we have lost the ability, as well as the willingness, to discriminate between the real and the sham.

Extravagant Expectations

While Boorstin establishes contemporary journalism as the prime purveyor of pseudo-events, he locates blame for this development with us, the American people. We have extravagant expectations of what the world holds, as well as of our power to shape the world. "By harboring, nourishing, and ever enlarging our extravagant expectations we create the demand for the illusions with which we deceive ourselves" (p. 5). This is a kind of "national self-hypnosis" (p. 3)—"Our seeming ability to satisfy our exaggerated expectations makes us forget that they are exaggerated" (p. 44). The result is that "the American citizen . . . lives in a world where fantasy is more real than reality, where the image has more dignity than its original."

The Graphic Revolution

For Boorstin, the media are more than mere purveyors of pseudo-events, created and disseminated in relation to news processes, responding to the demands of an illusioned public that expects too much. Such a view would be more like Macdonald's, with his "reciprocating engine" of production and consumption of mass culture. Macdonald ultimately locates the desire for mass culture in the social relationships of a disconnected mass society; in contrast, Boorstin ultimately locates the desire for illusions in a technological process—the new means of image reproduction.

For Boorstin, the mass media are an aspect of a larger historical process, which he terms "the Graphic Revolution." This revolution has been the immense increase, in modern times, in our ability to make, preserve, transmit, and disseminate precise images. Boorstin treats the mass media as an aspect of a longer history of image representation, including the printing press, engraving, lithography, photography, film, and television. Boorstin defines the media, broadly, as new technologies of *images*, technologies that have novel powers and deleterious consequences.

There is, he argues, a "diabolical irony" in this increasing capability. Our technological advances underlie our decline, our progress undermines our future, our hopes create our despair:

> The very facsimiles of the world which we make on purpose to bring it within our grasp, to make it less elusive, have transported us into a new world of blurs. By sharpening our images we have blurred all our experience. (p. 213)

The Thicket of Unreality

Boorstin addresses the dominance of pseudo-events in our contemporary lives. He connects this dominance both to journalism as practiced in an age of easy and sophisticated image reproduction and to a public that (unaware of any deception) demands exciting, stimulating, and comforting illusions over (comparatively) dull reality. In his terms, "we have used our wealth, our literacy, our technology, and our progress, to create the thicket of unreality which stands between us and the facts of life" (p. 3).

But what is this "thicket of unreality" that "we" have created? How is our experience blurred? First, it is fundamentally blurred by the loss of our ability and our desire to distinguish between reality and illusion. This process is described using the now familiar metaphor of food consumption:

> Once we have tasted the charm of pseudo-events, we are tempted to believe they are the only important events. Our progress poisons the sources of our experience. And the poison tastes so sweet that it spoils our appetite for plain fact. (p. 44)

Charmed, tempted, and poisoned, we take seriously staged forms like presidential debates and created news events. The tragic consequence of this is that our experience becomes tautological, a house of mirrors. "The vacuum of our experience is actually made emptier by our anxious straining with mechanical devices to fill it artificially" (p. 60).

Tourism becomes an implicit metaphor, for Boorstin, of the "diluted, contrived, prefabricated" nature of modern experience (p. 79). Tourism is the modern usurper of the premodern activity of travel. Travel was once, Boorstin claims, active, strenuous, and exploratory. In contrast, tourism is passive, a spectator sport where we expect events and preimagined happenings. "The tourist's appetite for strangeness . . . seems best satisfied when the pictures in his own mind are verified in some far country." Tourists in contemporary experience, with minds full of prefabricated images, we are insulated from reality, unaware of the house of mirrors in which we have chosen to live.

Dissolving Forms

The paradox that most troubles Boorstin is that, while the Graphic Revolution multiplied and vivified our images of the world, it did not sharpen or clarify the visible outlines of the world. Instead, the new images blurred our distinctions, leaving us in a shapeless, empty, meaningless world. Boorstin's primary concern is with the distinctions between sham and reality, but other blurrings also worry him.

Like Macdonald, Boorstin seeks to protect a distinction between art and nonart. Boorstin discusses the popularization of art as a process that has "garbled, emended, watered down, taken out of context" artistic works (p. 120). Echoing Macdonald, Boorstin believes that popularization attempts to make art, "which had the power somehow to remain uniquely itself, and itself alone" (p. 119) into something that is "interesting" or "edifying" or "amusing" or "instructive."

The Graphic Revolution not only reshapes and disembodies works of art, he claims, thus blurring the distinctions between art and nonart, but it also dissolves and makes interchangeable specific cultural forms. Thus the novel becomes a movie, a painting becomes a poster becomes advertising, a play becomes a celebrity showcase, the author becomes a personality.

Similarly, "we" blur the distinctions between celebrities and heroes, unaware of the crucial differences between them. For Boorstin, heroes are genuine, known for their deeds, while celebrities are, in his memorable phrase, "known primarily for their well-knownness" (p. 65). Our consciousness is "overpopulated" (p. 53) and "diluted" (p. 54) by celebrities, "human pseudo-event[s], fabricated on purpose to satisfy our exaggerated expectations of human greatness." Celebrities, like all pseudo-events, become "receptacles into which we pour our own purposelessness" (p. 61).

Our purposelessness is connected to a further blurring between the image—synthetic, believable, passive, vivid, simplified, and ambiguous—and the "already there" ideal, created by tradition, history, or God. Images have come to replace ideals, leaving us—personally and as a society—unable to strive actively toward them. For Boorstin, "Images are the pseudo-events of the ethical world. They are at best only pseudo-ideals. They are created and disseminated in order to be reported, to make a 'favorable impression.' Not because they are good, but because they are interesting" (pp. 243-244).

The dangerous consequence of all this blurring is that "in a world of dissolving moral and aesthetic forms, man the self-maker displaces them all. But his figure, too is a figment" (p. 168). Boorstin claims we come to believe that *all* forms are interchangeable and, worse, that the world is ours to make and remake in our own (created) image. We become fascinated with appearances and with how images are constructed; we lose any desire to discriminate between the substance and the shadow.

The Menace of Unreality

Finally, then, our personal lives become monotonous, and (drawing again on the food image) "our tired palates will not let us find our way back" (p. 258). Boorstin quotes a nineteenth-century critic who called cheap novels "the chewing gum of the mind" and a later critic who called television "chewing gum for the eyes." He suggests that "the Graphic Revolution has offered us the means of making all experience a form of mental chewing gum, which can be continually sweetened to give us the illusion that we are being nourished" (p. 258).

As our personal lives become pallid and enervating, our public lives and aspirations become specious quests to "live up to images," to match the pseudo-event (public opinion polls, images of success, celebrities) with our extravagant expectations:

> Nearly everything we do to enlarge our world, to make life more interesting, more varied, more exciting, more vivid, more "fabulous," more promising, in the long run has an opposite effect. In the extravagance of our expectations and in our ever increasing power, we transform elusive dreams into graspable images within which each of us can fit. By doing so we mark the boundaries of our world

with a wall of mirrors. Our strenuous and elaborate efforts to enlarge experience have the unintended result of narrowing it. In
frenetic quest for the unexpected, we end by finding only the unex-
pectedness we have planned for ourselves. We meet ourselves coming back. (p. 255)

In summary, then, Boorstin seeks an escape from this "plague,
our disease of extravagant expectations" (p. 259). He suggests
that the only cure is to recognize the disease, to realize that we
have been sleepwalking, to "discover anew where dreams and
where illusions begin." He ends his book by saying, "The least
and the most we can hope for is that each of us may penetrate
the unknown jungle of images in which we live our daily lives"
(p. 261).

Boorstin's argument is founded on the positing of a "real
world" that can be (and once was) directly experienced and
known. The new technologies of image reproduction appeared
to increase direct experience and knowledge, but instead
they diverted, prevented, and finally came to substitute for it.
Media-disseminated images stand between us and "reality,"
and until we recognize the deception, we remain in a tautological world of blurred distinctions and empty experience.

But was the world ever really directly apprehended? Is there
a way to experience without interpretation? A counterargu-
ment to Boorstin's assumptions of the possibility of seeing the
world directly is to suggest that all perceptions, even scientific
ones, are at some level "fictions." Even a factual account is a
form of narrative, constructed to "make sense" of perceptions.

Further, one could argue that our pretechnological history
is chock-full of preplanned events, rituals, ceremonies, celebra-
tions—that there never was a premodern time free from created narratives. Rather than seeing these premodern "pseudo-
events" as illusions and sham, anthropologists believe them to
be crucial modes of being-in-the-world, modes that sustain
meaning in human life.

Is it inevitably dangerous to believe in images, or is it the origin and intent of those images that should concern us? Boorstin's argument proceeds in ways that make it difficult to separate "good" images from "bad," beyond implying that there are such things as factual renderings of natural events, and that they alone are worthy of widespread attention and belief.

Finally, and most crucially, Boorstin believes in the inherent goodness of "facts." But what, exactly, is the therapeutic power of facts, and what, exactly, is the enervating power of fantasy? Boorstin's argument hinges, at its deepest level, on making a distinction between "natural" and "cultural." He assumes the inherent benevolence of the given (natural) and the inherent untrustworthiness of the human-made (cultural). This nature/culture tension recurs in media commentary and represents another unresolved contradiction in the media/modernity critique.

Ewen, too, sees a "thicket of unreality" being purveyed by the media, but he does not see this thicket as automatically evolving in connection with improved technological capacities. For Ewen, the media-based unreality is ideological, a "consumer culture" grounded in capitalism and directly serving its needs. Ewen is concerned not with the existence of images, but with the purposes to which images are put.

Consumer culture not only hides the realities of economic oppression, Ewen argues, it actively promotes faith in product consumption as a modern, democratic panacea. The central problem, in Ewen's analysis, is still "illusion," but what is at stake is very different. Boorstin wants us to experience the world directly and fully, and to learn to recognize and protect distinctions; Ewen wants us to recognize the inequities of corporate capitalism and to learn how to gain control of both the means of production and the means of image reproduction.

Stuart Ewen:
The Media as Ideological Apparatus

In *Captains of Consciousness: Advertising and the Social Roots of the Consumer Culture,* Stuart Ewen (1976) addresses advertising as the primary form of modern consumer culture, a culture that creates and sustains an ideology of consumption. This ideology not only obscures the real relations of capitalism, it also defuses the unrest that industrial inequity generates. By equating consumption with freedom and democracy with capitalism, the ideology of consumption promotes a loyalty to capitalism that is self-sustaining. We work to buy, and cannot question, even come to celebrate, this system that makes sense of inhumane working conditions, because it makes possible more purchases of unnecessary products.

Advertising creates a "spectacle of change" (p. 87) as it touts new products, improved technologies, and seasonal styles. Consumption becomes specious participation in change, because it offers a neutralized mode of action that cannot possibly alter the fundamental relationship between individuals and the corporate order. Consumption becomes the alternative to other modes of social action; it mobilizes industrial frustration and boredom in ways that maintain the order that generates it.

Advertising, the vehicle of consumer culture, penetrates our personal lives, Ewen argues, refiguring our beliefs about ourselves, our families, our friends, our homes, our past, present, and future. "The logic of . . . advertising read[s], one can free oneself from the ills of modern life by embroiling oneself in the maintenance of that life" (p. 44). In other words, advertising, via an ideology of consumption, portrays products as redemptive purchases, thus even more closely allying unsatisfied workers with the very system that oppresses them.

Captains of Industry/Captains of Consciousness

Ewen's central argument is that mass culture is *not* a self-generating process—it does not innocently "evolve" as a modern cultural realm. It is a form of social control, devised to serve the needs of industry for a stable work force and a predictable, homogeneous consumer market. The captains of industry, when faced in the late nineteenth century with increased production capabilities and a rebellious work force, promoted the development of a responsive consumer market and a docile work force by becoming "captains of consciousness," using advertising, via the mass media, to persuade workers to "work to buy."

"Mass culture" is Ewen's term for modern, mediated culture—it is suffused with the ideology of consumption, for which advertising is the primary, but not the sole, vehicle. Most media content, apparently, is mass culture—advertising is the most concentrated form of a more general cultural pattern grounded in the needs of industrial, now corporate, capitalism.

The ideology of consumption obscures the industrial production process, because it "denies not only the reality of human participation in production, but also the ability of human understanding to comprehend their mystified Nature. Within such a world, the product takes on a mysterious reality impervious to the understanding or action of the population" (p. 105). It thus deflects radical action, cultivating a misplaced loyalty to the industrial order.

Defining the Social Realm

The key to defining a social order that can support the demands of the production process, while neutralizing opposition to it, is to conflate consumption with all aspects of human experience. In other words, an ideology of consumption must penetrate all aspects of contemporary life, developing an insidious naturalness that makes it appear worthy, appropriate, "right."

Ewen details the ways in which he believes media-dissem-inated ideology comes to define the social realm. He traces an ever more powerful penetration of the ideology of consumption into contemporary life, grounding his analysis in the expressed goals of the developing advertising and public relations indus-tries and early twentieth-century advertisements.

In the 1920s, Ewen claims, advertising promoted itself as a "civilizing" influence, capable of achieving national homoge-neity, and thus unity (p. 92). Advertising adopted a nationalist, democratic language, conflating patriotism with product con-sumption, offering immigrants ways to assimilate and workers ways to achieve the American Dream, now defined as product ownership.

Advertising "civilizes the self" by scrutinizing the body for "uncivilized" smells, shapes, sizes, and colors, and offering products to eradicate all that is potentially offensive. It offers "mass produced visions of individualism by which people could extricate themselves from the mass" (p. 45). In other words, it paradoxically offers individual transcendence only through participation in mass consumption.

In Ewen's analysis, the family unit becomes a particular ideological site—the wage earner is made to feel, via the ideol-ogy of consumption, that working for money to buy products is what "providing for the family" involves. Patriarchy is recon-stituted in capitalism, rather than challenged. The father is made to associate his job and his wage-earning ability with social prestige; in the home his social authority is replaced by a kind of commercial authority—how good a product provider is he?

At the same time, according to Ewen, bureaucratic ideals of efficiency and organization are offered to the housewife, thus allying her with corporate values in her own home. And finally, children become conduits of the new ideology, bringing home from school, the YMCA, movies, and other modern cultural forms the industrialized moralities that argue for an expanded realm of consumption.

Commercializing Expression

Ewen concentrates on the ideological impact of advertising—its influence on people's values and beliefs—rather than on the impact of mass mediation on high culture (as does Macdonald) or on our ability to discriminate truth from illusion (as Boorstin does). Nonetheless, he devotes a chapter to the "realm of artistic creativity," where the "organization of objects and the dissolution of the subject took perhaps its most obvious toll" (p. 61).

What concerns Ewen are the demise of localized cultures and traditional arenas of creative expression, and the "artistic strangulation" (p. 66) of the creative worker by the marketplace. These are connected—artists are conscripted by the industrial machine and, once participating, contribute to the "eradication of indigenous cultural expression and the elevation of the consumer marketplace to the realm of an encompassing 'Truth' " (p. 67).

Participation in this commercial manipulation causes "anguish" in the artist—Ewen cites Sherwood Anderson, Wallace Stevens, and James Rorty as ex-admen who felt that their artistic abilities had been "conscripted and deformed" by the commercial system. Ewen does not explore how, exactly, commerce deforms or strangles art—his brief analysis merely references critiques of commercialization by early twentieth-century writers. Ewen's analysis depends on an assumption that commerce and art are inherently separate realms, and that commerce inevitably poisons and deforms art. This art/commerce distinction is yet another common, and virtually unquestioned, assumption in media criticism.

Control of the Social Realm

The abiding concern in Ewen's analysis is with the loss of our ability to recognize our own true needs and to speculate on the solutions to those needs. We cannot truly determine the conditions of our existence, because the media-based ideology of consumption mystifies the fundamental relations of capitalism. We cannot begin to find a solution to our dissatisfaction because the only solutions offered are ones that promote the ultimate cause of our unhappiness. The cure feeds the disease, and contemporary Americans are duped into support of a system that is not in their own best interests.

Ewen's argument, like the arguments of many other twentieth-century social critics, depends on a view of recent history as the change from agrarian community to industrial society. This is the account of modernity that is the implicit context of media commentary; it will be discussed more fully in Chapter 2.

Ewen and other social critics suggest that once the bonds of community, custom, and "traditional" modes of life dissolved, there was an implicit window of opportunity for a new kind of egalitarian and participatory industrial democracy. This opportunity was subverted by the captains of industry, and they have been able to protect their power by becoming captains of consciousness. Ewen's ultimate purpose is to explain how and why American workers acted and continue to act in ways that are not in their own best interests.

In summary, Ewen argues that the ideology of consumption is the means by which capitalism secures the consent, even the enthusiastic support, of the oppressed. The media are inherently manipulative ideological apparatuses, serving the needs of the corporate order for control of the social realm.

Ewen's argument assumes an inherent contradiction between the purposes of art and the purposes of commerce. The persuasive power of his case requires belief in the inherently corrupting influence of commerce on art and on consciousness. A particular system of commerce, capitalism, has been thoroughly critiqued as an inherently alienating economic system. But in Ewen's work, as in that of other critics, "commerce" and "commercialization" are seen as inherent evils, without necessarily referring to Marxist theory. There is widespread mistrust of commercialization, without much analysis of what this process is or how it operates.[5]

Ewen's argument also presupposes a "real" social foundation of economic relations that is obscured by ideology. But are economic relations the real basis of society? This orthodox Marxist position has been reframed, particularly in relation to the ways in which ideology operates; the "social formation" is more complicated than, perhaps, traditional Marxist analyses allowed.[6]

Does ideology inevitably obscure? Like Boorstin, Ewen must assume that there are "right" ways to see the "real" world and that there is a bewitching fog (ideological rather than pseudorepresentational) that has us in its grip. If this is so, explanations are needed for how Ewen (among others) escapes its powers. Explanations of how critics escape the fog that bewitches the masses usually suggest critical facility and theoretical sophistication as amulets against false consciousness, but this risks an elitism that can, or should, be discomfiting in American thought.

Ewen equates capitalism with oppression and media content with ideology. Thus capitalism must be deemed inevitably oppressive and always against humans' "true needs." This is an article of faith from the Left, but it is not irrefutable; oppression comes in many forms, and capitalism may, perhaps, have unrecognized possibilities.

Ewen assumes media content is mass culture, mass culture is capitalist culture, and capitalist culture is inevitably univocal. But does all media content always say, to everyone, "Work to buy and therefore to be happy"? By presuming that media = mass culture = capitalist culture, Ewen must claim a monolithic force that cannot easily be challenged, subverted, or even misunderstood. The audience is believed to be in the thrall of capitalist ideology, as purveyed in mass culture via the media.

Most of what Ewen deplores resonates with popular critics across the political spectrum—one need not speak from the Left to deplore the commercialization of expression, the corrosive influences of advertising, and the dangers of the modern consumption ethos. The Marxist critique that undergirds his argument, however, has been challenged by others as overly con-spiratorial or doctrinaire. There can be wholehearted agree-ment among critics about the "badness" of media without agreement about the political or economic or social theories that justify the belief.

Mainstream American media criticism maintains an uneasy faith in the possibility of economic and cultural improvement. Reform rather than revolution is what is usually advocated. The hope is that, somehow, the public will become aware of the dangers of "unworthy" media, and will demand (and thus get) "better" media. The hope is that, through exhortation, the pub-lic can learn to recognize its own best interests. These are the interests that the critic already sees, and wants the people, and the media, to act in relation to.

This seems to be the underlying purpose of Postman's book, which assumes that "we" are losing the ability to recognize and act in our own best interests, due to the deleterious influences of the mass media. Postman offers an apocalyptic view of national media enchantment and implies, like Boorstin, that we must shake ourselves awake if we are to be saved.

Neil Postman:
The Media as Corrosive Amusement

The title of Postman's book, *Amusing Ourselves to Death* (1985), crystallizes his central claim. He argues that television transforms everything it touches, trivializing serious forms of public discourse (like news, politics, science, education, com-merce, and religion) by turning them into entertainment. We, the public, are unwittingly drawn to this trivialized entertain-ment and are transformed by it.

For Postman, the dominant image is one of corrosion by technology—the print-based epistemology (on which liberal democracy was founded) is now being threatened via a danger-ous new television epistemology. This new epistemology is one that will harm us, because (in the guise of amusement) it thwarts logic, reason, and good sense. Under its influence, we will amuse ourselves to death.

Like Macdonald, Boorstin, and Ewen, Postman grounds his argument in an assumed historical transformation. In his case, it is a transformation from a print-based society to a television-based society. He believes that "the media of communication available to a culture are a dominant influence on the formation of the culture's intellectual and social preoccupations" (p. 9).[7] For Postman, print supports a serious, coherent, and rational culture, while television supports a "shriveled" and "absurd" "peek-a-boo" world.

It is Postman's assertion that "the printed page revealed the world, line by line, page by page, to be a serious, coherent place, capable of management by reason, and of improvement by logical and relevant criticism" (p. 62). "I hope to persuade you," he writes, "that the decline of a print-based epistemology and the accompanying rise of a television-based epistemology has had grave consequences for public life, that we are getting sillier by the minute" (p. 24).

Postman supports his claim by arguing that public discourse in the age of print was serious and rational. He uses the Lincoln-Douglas debates as a touchstone example—he claims that, there, the arguments were carefully and logically developed and that the audience had a long attention span and was "made up of people whose intellectual lives and public businesses were fully integrated into their social worlds" (p. 47). The audience was made up of "typographic men," who were detached, analytical, and devoted to logic, and who abhorred contradictions (p. 57). They had a sophisticated ability to think conceptually, deductively, and sequentially (p. 63).

These characteristics and abilities are based in a chronic engagement with the printed page, Postman believes, which means

> to follow a line of thought, which requires considerable powers of classifying, inference-making and reasoning. It means to uncover

lies, confusions and overgeneralizations, to detect abuses of logic and commonsense. It also means to weigh ideas, to compare and contrast assertions, to connect one generalization to another. To accomplish this, one must achieve a certain distance from the words themselves, which is, in fact, encouraged by the isolated and impersonal text. (p. 51)

In contrast, engagement with television "abandons logic, reason, sequence, and rules of contradiction" (p. 105). The telegraph, Postman claims, served as the catalyst for the shift from "The Age of Exposition" (print-based) to "The Age of Show Business" (television-based). He suggests that the telegraph introduced three "demons of discourse": irrelevance, impotence, and incoherence.

Irrelevance is assured because the telegraph, like later forms of electronic communication, can bear a large volume of context-free information, disconnected from the people it addressed. Impotence follows because, in this glut of context-free information, there is a low information/action ratio—most of what we know is "inert, consisting of information that gives us something to talk about but cannot lead to any meaningful action" (p. 68). Finally, telegraphy supports incoherence through its "sensational, fragmented, impersonal" language (p. 70) that depicts an "unmanageable, even undecipherable" world (p. 68).[8]

Thus, for Postman, it is telegraphy, rather than Boorstin's Graphic Revolution, that begins the assumed decline. Nonetheless, he approvingly incorporates Boorstin's arguments in *The Image* by combining telegraphy and photography into a force that supports what he calls a "pseudo-context,"

a structure invented to give fragmented and irrelevant information a seeming use. But the use the pseudo-context provides is not action, or problem-solving, or change. It is the only use left for information with no genuine connection to our lives. And that, of course, is to amuse. The pseudo-context is the last refuge . . . of a culture overwhelmed by irrelevance, incoherence and impotence. (p. 77)

Amusement is dangerous not in and of itself, but when it penetrates inherently serious forms of public discourse, and becomes the world in which we live:

> There is nothing wrong with entertainment. As some psychiatrist once put it, we all build castles in the air. The problems come when we try to *live* in them. The communications media of the late nineteenth and early twentieth centuries, with telegraphy and photography at their center, called the peek-a-boo world into existence, but we did not come to live there until television. (pp. 77-78)

Television, then, is "the command center of the new epistemology," from which there is no escape:

> There is no audience so young that it is barred from television. There is no poverty so abject that it must forgo television. There is no education so exalted that it is not modified by television. And most important of all, there is no subject of public interest—politics, news, education, religion, science, sports—that does not find its way to television. Which means that all public understanding of these subjects is shaped by the biases of television. (p. 78)

Like Boorstin and Ewen, Postman is concerned with how readily and completely we have adjusted to the new media environment. The "bizarre" and "disconnected" world of television has come to seem natural to us, he believes. We see irrelevant things as filled with import, and believe incoherence to be "eminently sane" (p. 80). Aldous Huxley's dystopic vision, in *Brave New World*, of "a people who come to love their oppression, and adore the technologies that undo their capacities to think" is fast approaching.

By making entertainment the "natural format" for the representation of all experience (p. 87), Postman argues, television presumes that everything is for our amusement and pleasure. This is evidenced in television news, in the ways in which it shifts from information fragment to information fragment ("Now . . . this") with cheerful banter, attractive newscasters, and appealing music. Show-business values like "visual interest" dominate television news, turning it into "a stylized dramatic performance" (p. 103).

Religion, too, becomes an entertainment. In religious broadcasting "everything that makes religion an historic, profound and sacred human activity is stripped away; there is no ritual, no dogma, no tradition, no theology, and above all, no sense of spiritual transcendence." Television has a strong bias to the secular, because it is so "saturated with our memories of profane events, so deeply associated with the commercial and entertainment worlds" (p. 119).

Political campaigns have become a series of 30-second spots, promoting image politics in a kind of therapeutic "feel good" mode. Similarly, education competes with the "curriculum" of television, a curriculum that is nongraded, inclusive, simplistic, and nonexpositional—the opposite of the sequential, continuous, exclusive perplexities Postman believes are offered in a print-based system.

Postman concludes his analysis by contrasting George Orwell's vision, in *1984*, of an imprisoning culture, dependent on censorship and thought control, with Aldous Huxley's vision of a burlesqued culture, where there is no need for censorship, wardens, or gates, because we have happily chosen our own spiritual devastation.

> When a population becomes distracted by trivia, when cultural life is redefined as a perpetual round of entertainments, when serious public conversation becomes a form of baby-talk, when, in short, a people become an audience and their public business a vaudeville act, then a nation finds itself at risk: culture-death is a clear possibility. (pp. 155-156)

Postman's analysis depends on a number of unexamined presuppositions. First, he argues for a pretelegraphic Eden, a time when politics, religion, and news were serious, rational, coherent, and logical, when people were, under the influence of print, also serious, rational, coherent, and logical. Was there such a time? If so, how do we explain the political spectacle, the broadsides and mudslinging and campaign songs of pretelegraphic America?

Postman also assumes a kind of content-free influence of print, disconnected from meaning. For him, print is *inherently* linear and logical, *automatically* cultivating serious habits of mind and modes of content. He makes this assertion, but gives no explanation for how form determines perception in this uniform way. Further, Postman's argument assumes that print demands some separate, previously extant category—rationality—and that television demands its dark twin—irrationality. Are these aspects of thought out there waiting for cultivation? Or are they called into being by the communication form? If so, once again, how does form determine these characteristics of thought?

Complicated issues of how communication works are ignored. Is content inevitably subsumed by form—is satire unamusing when written? Is a funeral automatically amusing when broadcast? The relationships among technology, culture, communication, and meaning are understood, in Postman's argument, to be simple and uncontradictory.

In his concrete examples of the ways in which television trivializes public discourse, Postman concentrates on content rather than form. Yet his early arguments are based on the televisual experience, the *how* of television, rather than on the content or meanings, the *what* of television. He implies that the "how" determines the "what," but does not explain how this happens—what is it about the visual/aural televisual process that promotes irrationality and amusement; what is it about the print/visual experience that makes it rational and serious?

The notion of art or literature is conspicuously absent from Postman's analysis—he seems uninterested in any self-consciously creative uses of media, including film, typography, phonography, and broadcasting. The artful uses of media to engage the emotions, to enchant, move, amuse, distract, are virtually unmentioned, except when these uses are applied to news, politics, religion, and education.

His argument relies on a belief that these spheres are naturally or inherently separate from artistic engagement and emotional response. Again we have the positing of necessary and "real" boundaries that are being blurred, as if those things called news, politics, religion, and education are natural forces that must, if they are to be valuable, remain uncontaminated.

Postman's argument requires an unquestioned dichotomy between serious and amusing, between rational and irrational, between coherent and fragmented, as well as the maintenance of iron clad distinctions between them. Postman seems to be arguing that entertainment is acceptable *in its place*, but that when it moves into inherently serious spheres, it trivializes and banalizes them. This argument is similar to the one made by Macdonald about mass culture when it moves into the sphere of art, by Boorstin about illusion when it masquerades as "reality," and by Ewen about commerce when it becomes the basis for social relations. All four authors make assumptions about pure spheres, arguing for their protection from pollution by outside influences. These influences, they argue, are media based.

Macdonald, Boorstin, Ewen, Postman: What the Media Do

The four authors discussed above make four distinct arguments about the nature of media influence. Macdonald is concerned about the fate of art (High Culture), and focuses on the role of the media in creating and disseminating Midcult and Masscult, which threaten art. For Macdonald, the media are disseminators of banal and trivial cultural forms; in this dissemination they cultivate us as banal and trivial people, increasingly unable to distinguish the culturally worthy from the culturally unworthy. The primary influence of the media is aesthetic, on the nature and quality of dominant cultural forms, and on our ability to recognize and respond to them.

Boorstin is concerned about the fate of reality, and he focuses on the role of the media in creating and disseminating illusions. For Boorstin, the media are creators and disseminators of pseudo-events; in this dissemination they cultivate us as befuddled wanderers in a hall of mirrors, increasingly unable to distinguish the real from the sham. The primary influence of the media is cognitive, on our ability to recognize and respond to "real life."

Ewen is concerned about the fate of social relations in the modern age, and he focuses on the role of media in disseminating a capitalist ideology of consumption. For Ewen, the media are ideological vehicles, cultivating us as passive consumers; given this cultivation, we are increasingly unable to distinguish between what is in our interests and what is in the interests of the oppressive system. The primary influence of the media is ideological, on our ability to recognize, and then act on, our own real needs and desires.

Postman is concerned about the fate of reason, logic, and coherence in the modern age, and he focuses on the role of television in trivializing public discourse by turning it into entertainment. For Postman, television is a pervasive epistemology that cultivates us as distractible amusements seekers; after this cultivation we are increasingly unable to develop logical, coherent understandings. The primary influence of the media is on public discourse, on our ability to conduct our common life in rational and logical ways.

For all four authors, then, the media corrode what is deemed an important or valuable aspect of life—art, reality, radical action or public discourse. Art (for Macdonald) offers a communal emotional catharsis, a valuable aesthetic experience, a sharing of worthy sensibilities. The media somehow banalize art, offering an ersatz culture in its place. Reality (for Boorstin) offers direct, unmediated, trustworthy experience; it is challenging and strenuous. The media somehow blur reality, offering distracting sham accounts in its place.

Radical change (for Ewen) requires consciousness of the real conditions of existence. This "unfalse" consciousness has the possibility of creating an egalitarian, participatory culture, one that addresses the true needs of its citizens. The media offer a deceptive account of the real relations of capitalism, creating false loyalty and subverting liberating action.

Rationality, when employed in public discourse, will support (for Postman) linear, coherent public discussion and understanding. The media offer amusing, fragmented accounts, transforming our public discourse into irrational baby talk.

Media as Transformative Power

How do the media manage to corrupt these valuable spheres of art, reality, true consciousness, and rationality? The answer to this question is at two levels—they either transform the thing itself (art becomes Midcult; public discourse becomes amusement) or they transform our *perceptions* of the thing, and thus they transform us. The most convincing claims of media power include this double punch.

The transformation of the thing itself usually involves some kind of tainting, through the combining of the pure with the corrupt. For Macdonald, art and Masscult, through "unnatural intercourse," yield a bastard child, Midcult. Therefore, if Art and Masscult were to remain separate and distinct spheres, art would remain aesthetically uncorrupted.

Similarly, Postman argues that rational public discourse and entertainment are mutually exclusive categories—television, by turning discourse into entertainment, pollutes rationality. If public discourse could remain in the print-based epistemology, untainted by the fragmentary power of entertaining television, then public discourse would remain uncorrupted.

The media not only somehow transform the thing itself, they also have the power to transform our own perceptions, desires, and tastes. According to all four authors, the media change us by offering something that is somehow more appealing, easier to "digest," than the good stuff: Masscult is more appealing that art; pseudo-events are more interesting than reality; product consumption is easier than radical change; amusing accounts are preferable to serious ones. We become corrupted by this exposure and not only forget how to tell "good" from "bad," but start wanting the stuff that is bad for us.

These analyses presume that we, the media audience, have some instinctual desire for stuff that is "bad for us." What the critics deem to be worthy is, apparently, always less interesting and desirable than the unworthy forms. Is there something inherently distasteful about "good stuff" and inherently de-lightful about "bad stuff"? If so, why would these critics want to force distasteful good stuff on us and deny us delightful bad stuff? Because, obviously, the "good" stuff *is* interesting and desirable, and thus preferable, to the critics themselves. These four authors see social as well as individual moral value in the "good stuff," and social as well as individual moral danger in the "bad stuff." What they are assuming is that what they themselves define as art, facts, true consciousness, or rational-ity can and will benefit us as individuals and as a society. Popular culture, dreams, capitalism, and amusement will harm us as individuals and as a society.

The Public as Media Victims

Why would we, the public, choose things that would harm us, and not choose things that will benefit us? At the heart of the media critique is an inescapable conundrum about public taste. For these media critics, "the people" are not choosing the cultural forms that would improve them and their common situation. Are we the people to be blamed? Are we to be cast, in American media criticism, as so tasteless, stupid, irrational, and malleable that we are unable to know what is best for us?

Of course not. This harsh view of "the people" is rarely offered in American criticism, from the Right or from the Left, at least not in such an unvarnished form. Still, "audience bashing" is a common, albeit obscured, undercurrent in media commentary. One way to avoid a direct attack on the people who are choosing the forms of culture or ideology or information or discourse that most disturb the critics is to blame the media for their effect on the audience. *Before* television, the Graphic Revolution, advertising or the Industrial Revolution (the argument goes), "the people" were serious, or recognized reality, or did not covet products, or responded to high aesthetic quality. Afterwards, with the full development of the mass media, the basically worthy people became somehow incapacitated.

If the people's inherent worthiness is not to be questioned, then the critic must argue that a basically intelligent, perceptive, discriminating audience is being seduced, manipulated, and befuddled by the media. *In short, a great deal of power must be ascribed to the media to explain why so many people are choosing to participate in such a dangerous and worthless practice.*

The media are thus endowed with seductive power. We as individuals are conceptualized as naturally drawn to the very junk that trivializes our taste, blurs our minds, subverts our desires, and destroys our reason. Media content (Macdonald, Boorstin, and Ewen) and media form (Postman) are such that they seduce us into affection for them—as Ewen and Postman explicitly argue, we come to love our oppressors.

The final destructive power of the medium, these authors argue, is in its ability to cultivate us in its own image—to turn us into itself. Once we have succumbed to its siren song, we become the worst of its qualities—aesthetically banal, cognitively confused, ideologically swaddled consumers who are (on top of everything else) epistemologically silly.

These critics make magical claims—the media turn art into trash, truth into illusion, action into passivity, reason into silliness. The media do this by offering us form and content so appealing that we cannot help but desire things that have terrible consequences for us individually and as a society. Once we spend time with the media we become like them—trivial, banal, illusioned, befogged, insatiable, and irrational. Stated this baldly, these charges of media influence sound grandiose, and more than a little paranoid. Yet we have seen how they inform the respected, often-quoted arguments of our four authors.

Despite the differences among the central charges, the basic structures of the criticism of all four authors is the same: There was once something pure and valuable in humankind and society that the media, by their form and/or content, can and will corrupt. We are unaware of this insidious effect, may even choose it, because the media seduce us into thinking we want what they have to offer. Once we have chosen the media, we become like them—corrupt and impure.

As we can see, the underlying structure of the media influence story is a mythic one. It is the story of the Garden of Eden, where a pure sphere was penetrated by the serpent, who seduced Eve into desiring the apple that forever tainted her (and us) with sin. It is also the myth of the Lorelei, monsters disguised as beautiful maidens whose tantalizing songs draw sailors off their course and to their doom.

Underlying the different arguments of Macdonald, Boorstin, Ewen, and Postman is the narrative structure that can be called the media influence story. This story offers us more than just a story of media influence, because it also tells a mythic tale of what once was, what is now, and what ought to be. By casting the media as an evil influence, we support a telling of the world wherein the past is mourned, the present is cursed, and the future is sure to be grim.

We need to consider the reasons for, and the consequences of, telling the story of media-in-society in this particular way. We also need to understand what the story tells us about our common life, and consider why it has been so convincing. In the following chapter an examination is presented of the ways in which the critique of modernity orients and justifies the media influence story.

Notes

1. Some representative collections of this array of arguments include Rosenberg and White (1957, 1971), Jacobs (1961), White (1970), and Lazere (1987).
2. Of particular usefulness are Hall and Whannel (1964), in their section "Mass Society: Critics and Defenders," and Gans (1974), in his chapter "The Critique of Mass Culture."
3. Dwight Macdonald's collection includes essays written between 1952 and 1962. The 75-page essay "Masscult & Midcult" is what I focus on here because it summarizes his media perspective. This essay was first published in the spring of 1960 in *Partisan Review*, but it builds on ideas developed earlier in "A Theory of Mass Culture," first published in *Diogenes* in 1953, and widely reprinted. Daniel J. Boorstin's book was originally published by Atheneum in 1961 as *The Image, or What Happened to the American Dream*, then was reprinted in paperback in 1972 as *The Image: A Guide to Pseudo-Events in America*.
4. Macdonald's essays originate in the early 1950s, Boorstin's in the late 1950s and early 1960s, Ewen's in the 1970s, and Postman in the 1980s.
5. I have explored the notion of commercialization in relation to country music production in Nashville in the 1950s (see Jensen, 1984, 1988). In the 1970s, some fans defined the 1950s as a period when country music became "big business," and considered the "Nashville sound" of the late 1950s and early 1960s to be "commercialized," in contrast to the more "authentic" honkytonk sound that preceded it. Interestingly, the Nashville sound is, in the 1980s, seen as less commercialized, and more authentic, than the 1960s and 1970s styles that succeeded it.
6. In media studies, this reformulation is accessible through Stuart Hall's work; see "Culture, Media, and the Ideological Effect" (Hall, 1979).
7. This assumption is developed in far more complexity and detail by Innis (1951, 1972), and reworked by his student McLuhan (1962, 1964), although neither makes or offers support for Postman's claim that electronic communication automatically supports a shriveled or absurd society.
8. For a very different view of the role of the telegraph in the emergence of mass communication see Carey's (1989) chapter, "Technology and Ideology: The Case of the Telegraph."

2

Media in Modernity

Macdonald, Boorstin, Ewen, and Postman are four voices that exemplify major aspects of American media discourse. In Chapter 3, the metaphoric patterns that inform their claims will be examined, but before going into more detail about media criticism in general, we need to explore the context in which it proceeds—the story of modernity.

In this chapter the criticism of modernity is considered in relation to the criticism of the mass media, demonstrating how the two discourses intersect. It will become clear that they share a narrative structure, one that depends on a myth of progress. Beliefs about the nature of the past, the present, and the future animate and orient media criticism. These beliefs need to be examined directly, in order to consider their usefulness in understanding the role of mass communication in contemporary life.

"Modernity," like "the media," is a sprawling concept. Considerations of it tend also to be vague and full of sweeping terms and evaluations. But the "modernity discourse" is amenable to summary, as a narrative, and to analysis, in relation to key conflicts or tensions. As the parallels between the critiques of the media and of modernity are identified, we can draw out points of tension, fault lines in the terrain. These fault lines suggest issues that deserve our attention and concern; they are issues that continue to surface in American social, cultural, and political thought.

The Possibility of Progress

The idea of progress underlies accounts of historical change. Change is evaluated in terms of advance or retreat: Is current life better or worse than in the past? Are we improving or declining? How can we, as a society, assure improvement and advance, and avoid decline and retreat?

The idea of progress sets up a narrative trajectory against which current life is evaluated. Offering the possibility of a "better world," either once existing in the past or potentially arriving in the future, it enables us to evaluate some social, cultural, and individual choices as "good" and others as "bad." We have a ready gauge of human social possibility, a gauge that can orient our discourse about media and contemporary life. But this gauge comes to us already value laden. It sets up the possibility of an "ideal" world, and then asks why it is not here with us now. Why have we either fallen from a former better state or failed to arrive at this state? What can explain why the world, today, is not as it once was or was once hoped to be?

This question animates social criticism, and implicitly orients media criticism. The mass media are defined as essentially modern phenomena, invented in the relatively recent past, and their influence is taken to be crucial to the characteristics of our age. When seeking to explain why we have either lost or failed to achieve an ideal world, the media become a logical scapegoat—were it not for the mass media, real progress would have been achieved.

A villain, the mass media, has been located in a simplistic narrative of beneficent social change—a villain that, some believe, had the potential to be a hero. One of the complexities of the media/modernity discourse is that the media can be both villain and potential hero—cast as both that which pollutes and that which could have saved. This duality is overlaid onto another duality—modernity as a loss of former grace and as the path to future grace. In this chapter I describe how these two dualities figure in the media/modernity discourse.

The Modernity Story

To many American social critics, modernity represents a betrayal of promise. Our society's development was supposed to be progressive—ever improving as humankind, freed from artificial constraints, became more rational, more informed, and more "civilized." Yet modern American life has not, at least to its critics, lived up to this promise. Instead, our contemporary life is seen as materially rich but spiritually impoverished. America is seen as being in cultural decline, in spite of, or even due to, its economic abundance.

"Modernity" exists only in relation to an assumed premodern time. The concept of "modernity" inevitably constructs a period before the host of changes that are defined as "modern." This "before-time" is usually called "premodern"; its character is seen as significantly different ("more traditional") from current times.

The term *modern* has become so widely and frequently applied to nineteenth- and twentieth-century culture and society that it no longer automatically references our current situation. This semantic dilution has supported the use of such terms as *postmodern* to describe contemporary culture and society.[1] Whatever the terminology employed, however, we still assume that we live in an age significantly different from the ages that preceded it, no matter what the label. For the current discussion, *modern* applies to the characteristics of contemporary culture and society (including those ascribed to postmodernism), and *premodern* refers to whatever is assumed to have preceded it.

In making a distinction between modern and premodern times, we are telling a story of major social and cultural change. We are assuming that there is a certain coherence to the change—the story of modernity implies a recognizable shift from one particular "age" to another.

The first problem in the construct of modernity is that its origins are ever receding. There is no firm agreement among historians, sociologists, anthropologists, cultural critics, and social critics about when, exactly, the "modern age" begins. Possible originating moments have included the 1920s, the turn of the century, and the late, middle, or early nineteenth century; but the Enlightenment and the Middle Ages have also been mentioned. Many technological innovations (printing press, cotton gin, factory system, steam engine, telegraph, radio, satellites, computers) have been hailed as precipitating the dawn of the modern age.

The complexity and fuzziness of the modernity concept is most acutely felt in international settings, when it is difficult to determine when and if a "developing" society has become "modernized," and whether this is a welcome or a dangerous change. The evaluation of international modernization depends in part on whether modernity is defined as urbanization, industrialization, bureaucratic organization, alienation, secularization, democratization, literacy, improved health care, technological advance, or some combination of these.

This conceptual fuzziness suggests that the defining characteristics of the modern are fluid, so that the premodern period (against which modernity is compared) also moves around in time. The supposed characteristics (and value) of modernity depend on a comparison to a premodern time, yet neither seems to have stable, agreed-upon referents. Nonetheless, the assumed characteristics of each remain stable—conceptually, "modernity" and "premodernity" are coherent, even if there is no agreed-upon time period to which they refer.

"Before" society is often called traditional society, so that "modern" and "traditional" refer to each other—whatever is characteristic of one is seen as absent or transformed in the other. Brown (1976) sets up contrasting "ideal types" of tradition and modernity, and shows how the story of modernity depends on the contrast. In Brown's ideal types, traditional society is stable, fixed, with little change from year to year. In contrast, modern society is unstable, fluid, with much change from year to year. Traditional societies are based in oral, face-to-face communication; modern societies in written and (later) electronic communication. Traditional societies are paternalistic and hierarchical, organized around kinship, while modern societies are bureaucratic and egalitarian, organized around social roles. Traditional societies interweave family and community in work, leisure, and religion, while modern societies define and distinguish among separate individuals who make distinctions between work and leisure and between sacred and secular.

This comparison of types is actually a story about the influence of the modern on the traditional (Bendix, 1970; Gusfield, 1967). The story of the relationship between tradition and modernity is that a static, normative, homogeneous society has been (or is being) weakened and overwhelmed by the mobile and heterogeneous modern. A cohesive community disintegrates under the fragmenting influence of the forces of modernity. In this telling, modernity is a loss of former grace.

We see, then, how modernity is predominantly conceptualized as a destructive outside influence—it is something that "happens to" an ongoing situation. This notion of outside influence is also the central theme of the story of media influence. Both the mass media and modernity are implicitly understood as being artificial "others" that invade, and subsequently transfigure, a natural circumstance.

Gusfield lists what he calls seven fallacies of this traditional/modern polarity. He criticizes the dominant theory of modernity as setting up a fallacious narrative. Using his argument, we can briefly consider why the story of modernity is told in these ways.

Gusfield believes it is fallacious to assume, as does the modernity critique, that societies were once static and that traditional cultures are consistent and normative. The modernity critique assumes that traditional cultures have a homogeneous social structure, and that new ways replace the old. This means that the modern is conceptualized as in inevitable conflict with the traditional. Thus traditional and modern are defined as being mutually exclusive systems, and modernity is seen as something that weakens tradition. In short, Gusfield summarizes the premodern/modern distinction, in order to disrupt its logic.

Gusfield ultimately suggests that the concept of tradition functions as a legitimating principle, offering an ideology and a program of action for social critics and for national policies. To extrapolate, he shows how "tradition" offers a way to tell the story of modernity's corruption of innocence. If the premodern is deemed traditional, and traditional cultures and societies are deemed to be stable and coherent, and modernity is seen as disruptive of this stability and coherence, then we have a story of contamination. The pure sphere of tradition is tainted by the influences of the modern. In this telling, there remains a possibility of redemption, once the polluting influences of modernity are somehow neutralized.

We have seen how media discourse locates the mass media as a disruptive influence, contaminating contemporary life. I have also alluded to the ways in which the media are seen as potentially redeeming or neutralizing modernity—this will be the focus of the discussion, in Chapter 3, of underlying metaphors in media criticism. The media have become primary vehicles in a larger critique of modernity—this means that media discourse will always bear the tensions and duality of the discourse on modernity.

That the story of modernity engages a seduction and betrayal myth similar to the one found in Macdonald, Boorstin, Ewen, and Postman in no way refutes the possibility that a modern age has indeed replaced a premodern one in just these ways. It simply points out the narrativity of the modernity assumption, a narrativity it shares with media discourse. Eventually, we will consider whether this narrative of disruption and disintegration is the most appropriate way to tell the story of social change.

The Duality of Modernity

It is important to recognize that the story of modernity is not, in every case, a story of disintegration and decline. In fact, the vernacular story of modernity can be exactly the opposite—a story of escape from the confines of premodern life. This is the more popular American story of technological and intellectual progress—the story of how the constraints of tradition, the bonds of the past, have been thrown off, and a new, liberating culture and society have been allowed to develop. This is the story that many Americans tell in relation to our own historical origins, technological development, and standards of living.

The clearest way to illustrate this duality in the discourse of modernity is to consider the rural/urban tension that it reproduces. The story of modernity is, at one level, the story of a move from rural to urban life. How we think about these two sites reveals much about how we think about the processes of modernity. In comparing the values of the country and the city, we find an ambivalence that is represented in a double list of positive and negative qualities for each. The city can be seen as cosmopolitan, exciting, full of opportunity and possibility, but also as alienating, estranging, full of danger and despair. The country can be seen both as communal and restorative and as confining and stifling—what in one reading is valued is, in the opposite reading, deplored.

This duality of evaluation is evidenced in the ambiguity that still threads its way through American accounts of small-town life. Small towns are conceptualized as happy enclaves of neighborly support, but also as petty arenas of mean-spirited gossip, or backwaters of ignorance and barbarism. Metropolitan existence can be characterized as exciting, romantic, and liberating, but also as unfriendly, stressful, violent, and crime laden. There is no easy resolution of this duality, no simple way to decide if the anonymity of the city is liberating or alienating, the communal nature of the small town stifling or supportive, the pace of the city exciting or exhausting, the pace of the country relaxing or enervating.

The often-invoked "traditional values" can be seen as wellsprings of important truths (premarital celibacy, heterosexuality, monogamy) but also as cesspools of superstition (patriarchy, homophobia, repression of desires). There are unresolved contradictions in American social thought, tensions that are based in a dual perception of rural/urban and, congruently, premodern/modern.

Media discourse can imply that the mass media are to blame for whatever is inadequate about current life. The media either cause this inadequacy themselves, by deepening and extending the unworthy processes of modernity, or are responsible for current ills because they fail to promote the worthy possibilities that modernity offers. Either way, whether one is a cheerleader for or critic of modernity, the media can be castigated and deeper, more intractable issues can be avoided.

And yet, intractable problems can be repressed, but they cannot be forever ignored. The intractable issues of modernity continue to haunt media criticism. I am arguing that media criticism represents, at one level, a displaced critique of modern life. I believe that, in our media criticism, we are addressing, tangentially, furtively, and incompletely, our unresolved concerns about modernity.

Taking on "modernity" full force is daunting—it is, too obviously, an abstract narrative, with few direct referents, with precious little concreteness and specificity. By taking on "the media" instead, criticism can address the abstract construct "modernity" via a stand-in. Criticism can thereby avoid two moves that would be devastating in American social thought: directly attacking the worth of the public, and directly questioning the possibilities of mass democracy.

These contradictions are papered over in the critique of the media. The media can be blamed both for the current ills of modernity and for deflecting the future promise of modernity.

It is a no-win situation for the media—they either cause current evil or fail to allow the future good.

But the dominant media discourse offers a win-win situation for the critic, because he or she can escape the contradictions that remain unresolved in the modernity critique. Blame has been placed; a villain has been found. The dualities of perception, the unresolved tensions in evaluating social change, and thus in choosing social goals, issues that must be confronted, challenged, and worked through, are left untouched.

The media incorporate, and are incorporated by, modernity. Thus the media can be seen as emblematic of the ills of modernity (fragmented, alienating, distracting) or as seducing us away from the potential promise of modernity (making us emotional, irrational, seeking diversion and trashy entertainment, unable to discriminate between hype and logic). In either case, the media become modernity's scapegoat—the media are attacked for what is frightening about contemporary life.

What *is* frightening about contemporary life? In order to understand how criticism of modernity haunts media criticism, we need to explore further the kinds of claims being made about modern life. The best way to begin this exploration is to develop the concept of mass society that figures in conceptions of the media as mass culture.

The Modern as Mass Society

Mass society theory emerged in nineteenth-century European thought in relation to the study of what were called "folkways." As peasant life was perceived as being eclipsed, the study of "traditional culture"—songs, tales, dress, dance— emerged. Such study was an attempt to preserve ways of life that were seen as disappearing under the influence of an emerging mass society.

Thus, from its beginning, mass society theory posits previously extant traditional folk communities as being overwhelmed by a new kind of social relation—mass society. Folk-ways are characterized as communal, face-to-face, and based in rural and religious habits, while mass society is characterized as atomized, distanced, and based in urban and secular habits.

The concept of a mass society depends (as does the concept of modernity) on its opposition to a concept of traditional community. Mass society is seen as disrupting previous patterns and ties; it weakens and destroys the bonds and habits of tradition. Mass society is characterized by mass culture—forms of symbolic expression that emerge in this new, alienated, atomized, and secular urban world.

Thus metaphors of breakdown and disintegration define mass society theory from its very beginnings. The "story of modernity" (the corruption of innocence) becomes, in mass society theory, the story of the disintegration of community. Traditional communities are defined as having offered supportive, nurturing, authentic connection to its members. The emerging mass society can offer only evanescent, tenuous, unreliable, and ever-shifting relations.

One of the most concise summaries of the mass society argument can be found in Bell (1956). He is worth quoting at length because his summary combines various strains of European mass society theory into a coherent and inclusive account:

> The revolutions in transport and communication have brought men into closer contact with each other and bound them in new ways; the division of labor has made them more interdependent; tremors in one part of society affect all others. Despite this greater interdependence, however, individuals have grown more estranged from one another. The old primary group ties of family and local community have been shattered; ancient parochial faiths are questioned; few unifying values have taken their place. Most important, the critical standards of an educated elite no longer shape opinion or taste. As a result, mores and morals are in constant flux, relations among individuals are tangential or compartmentalized rather than organic.
>
> At the same time greater mobility, spatial and social, intensifies concern over status. Instead of a fixed or known status symbolized by

dress or title, each person assumes a multiplicity of roles and constantly has to prove himself in a succession of new situations. Because of all this, the individual loses a coherent sense of self. His anxieties increase. There ensues a search for new faiths. The stage is thus set for the charismatic leader, the secular messiah, who, by bestowing on each person the semblance of necessary grace, and of fullness of personality, supplies a substitute for the older unifying belief that the mass society has destroyed. (p. 75)

Notice how Bell's summary weaves together a number of claims, moving from cause (revolution in transportation and communications) to contradictions: greater interdependence but estrangement; freedom but anxiety; and, finally, to a terrifying outcome—the specter of a public vulnerable to a secular messiah.

Bell highlights the central claims of European mass society theory, as first developed in the nineteenth century by Tönnies, Durkheim, and Simmel, and later elaborated in the twentieth century by members of the Frankfurt School. Of greatest concern are the ultimate results of the "shattered" bonds of family, community, ethnicity, religion. The loss of organic coherence, both personal and social, results not only in a more anxious, less meaningful personal existence, but in a social vulnerability to totalitarianism.

Bell's summary is designed to support his subsequent critique of the concept of mass society as theoretically useless. He finds it to be illogical and without organizing principles. His criticism is justified, but he does not consider the reasons for these shortcomings. Mass society theory, in spite of its origins in intellectual and scholarly thought, was never a theory in the scientific sense of the term. It was, however, a conceptual model, a way of organizing thought. As such, it can be considered a social narrative, a discourse that has emerged in relation to particular historical circumstances. Social narratives lack the logic and organizing principles of "theory" because they emerge in response to experienced ambivalences and contradictions. They are not designed to be tested against particular empirical data, or refuted and reformulated to fit experimental findings. Rather, they are points of view, designed to make the contradictory social world coherent.

Social narratives, like those that tell the stories of modern society and of media influence, are rarely fully articulated or coherently defended at the theoretical level. Like ideology, they are "given." They need no logic or coherent structure because they need no defense—they are "obviously" true. These vernacular theories are illogical and without coherent organizing principles because they are negotiated truces, ways to tell stories that allow contradictions and ambivalences to continue without excessive discomfort.

There are obvious contradictions in the mass society theory, as developed by European theorists, especially when it is adopted in American thought. There is a nostalgic emphasis on the notions of "primary group ties" and "ancient parochial faiths," and barely suppressed longing for a feudal, aristocratic heritage ("critical standards of an educated elite," "fixed or known status symbolized by dress or title"). In European mass society theory, there is a yearning for both a perceived "authentic" folk life and a perceived "stable" hierarchy of authority.

These are characteristics of mass society theory that are especially problematic in American social thought. The "authentic folk life" of eighteenth-century America is not centuries-old peasant life, but at best a newly developed middle-class colonial life, or, in the nineteenth century, an emerging western pioneer life. Either nostalgicized eastern seaboard entrepreneurship or pioneer/cowboy life becomes the supposedly "authentic" American past that is being eclipsed.

These are relatively flimsy "traditional communities" to counterbalance the vision of an emerging mass society. They are obviously constructed ideals; they represent promise and possibility, not age-old folkways. In fact, they offer a characteristic American, and modern, vision of boosterism and the taming of the wilderness—there is a built-in excitement about the potential of "the new" in American beliefs about social change.

As Bramson (1961) points out, American social thought is based in a liberal, individualist heritage.[2] Because America is without a traditional past, social theorists must rework the mass society concept if they are to address American modernity. The European conception of mass society begins with an image of social disintegration based in the perceived loss of a traditional past; the American conception of mass society, and thus of modernity, cannot easily share those images.

American construction of a theory of modernity must contend with the fact that America was *deliberately* modern. If modernity is understood as being the loss of traditional bonds, as a repudiation of traditional hierarchies and practices, then America was founded to *be* modern.

America was founded in relation to Enlightenment beliefs about the nature of social contracts and natural laws. America's founding principles assume that, liberated from the bonds of class, ethnicity, and religion, autonomous, rational humankind would triumph, living in harmony with natural law. In short, modernity was a freedom from constraints that would allow the flourishing of natural goodness.

This colonial liberal heritage is reproduced in the settling of the West, where individuals and families invented communities to meet their own needs, and moved on if they did not. America is doubly conceived of as liberated from constraint; in both the colonial and western imagination it is an open, free space in which "natural man" can triumph.

But the open, free space of America became, as we know, a site of unrestrained industrialization and urbanization. Immigrants, shedding their ties to community, ethnicity, and class, came to America eager to participate in the promise of the urban, industrial nation. This makes a triply modern American heritage: a colonial faith in natural law, a western faith in individual mobility, and an immigrant faith in an egalitarian new world of opportunity.

The American heritage, then, is one of optimism, of potential, and of promise. Modernity can readily be seen as a positive force; it is progress in its richest, most beneficent form. Yet the nineteenth-century American heritage of optimism becomes increasingly undercut by pessimism as the twentieth century draws near; by the middle of the twentieth century the critique of American modern life, as mass society, is fully developed, heavily influenced by European social thought.

Thus the European critique of mass society, founded on the passing of defined folkways, concerned with the loss of aristocratic stratification and standards, finds an uneasy home in the American critique of modern life, founded on the promise of new beginnings, and concerned with individual freedom and possibility.

When we examine the twentieth-century critique of media and modernity, we find everywhere the evidence of tension between the promises and the actualities of American life. American conceptions address failed promise as well as lost traditions and consider threats to the success of the experiment as well as the dangers of changing old ways. In this way, the modernity critique, which is more single-edged in European approaches to mass society, is inevitably double-edged in American thought. We deplore loss as we trust change.

The ambivalence about modern life, in American social thought, is in relation to these unresolved tensions between mass society theory and American faith in progress. This is evidenced in the reworking of European conceptualizations to apply to the American situation, in the transformation of Durkheimian and Weberian concepts to speak to the American condition.

Similarly, Bramson suggests that mass communication research in the 1940s, 1950s, and 1960s was a characteristic American response to fears of mass society. In partial response to mass society theorists, American social scientists studied communication processes in relation to fears of propaganda and the manipulation of public opinion, and sought to prove that even modern Americans still lived, worked, and thought in primary groups. Thus modern American society was not the atomized and fragmented mass society of the Frankfurt School theorists, and totalitarianism could not triumph here.[3]

American Modernity

If America is deemed a "mass society," it is mainly in relation to dreams of a democratic utopia, rather than to memories of a feudal tradition. The nature of these utopian dreams, and the ways that a feudal European tradition still haunts them, can be explored using five "unit ideas" suggested by Nisbet (1966). These epitomize, for him, the general conceptual conflict between tradition and modernity. Nisbet uses the tensions between community and society, authority and power, status and class, sacred and secular, and alienation and progress to explore the development of sociology in both America and Europe. These unit ideas can help us describe how modernity is understood, in American commentary, in relation to the theory of mass society and the social narrative of media-in-society.

Community/Society

The community/society dichotomy references social relations. It implies that premodern life was marked by face-to-face, intimate relationships among friends, while modern life is characterized by distant, impersonal contact among strangers. Communities are defined as shared, close, and intimate, while societies are defined as separate, distanced, and anonymous. "Atomized" is the most common descriptor of relations in mass society—each individual operating separately, connected loosely if at all.

What is at stake in this dichotomy, in American social thought, is the issue of connection—how we are to link up with each other in America. Do the ties of family, religion, ethnicity, or geography bind us, a nation of recent immigrants to a new land? If these ties do not apply, what *does* connect us? Can patriotism or civic life flourish in a mobile, multicultural society? What kind of self is cultivated in an impersonal society? What kinds of loyalties, morals, and character can exist if one is born without communal values and experiences?

These are the unanswered questions and issues that most concern Bellah, Madsen, Sullivan, Swidler, and Tipton in *Habits of the Heart* (1985). In interviews with White middle-class Americans, these researchers found evidence for their own concerns over the relationship of the modern individual to community and to public life. They found a consistent yearning for meaning and coherence, a chronic nostalgia for a communal American past, and a rejection of what they call the "managerial and therapeutic ethos" of individual development in isolation from community.

The overall effect of modernity, Bellah et al. and other critics suggest, is to offer only weak and evanescent connections. The uprooted modern individual is seeking community, longing for coherence and reliable meaning, but unable to realize such a goal in a fragmented world of contradictory values. The modern individual is at risk, easily manipulated by charismatic leaders, swayed by propaganda, seduced by slick promises— in other words, at the mercy of the media, which can and will provide identity and connection, however specious and self-serving they may be.

It is this vision that haunts Ewen (1976) as he describes how the captains of consciousness have used advertising to offer an illusion—consumption—as a modern vehicle of community. As modern social relations, determined by the needs of capitalism, altered and deformed the American working class, consumer culture offers a false way to restore community. Products become the ways in which modern workers, made vulnerable by the loss of authentic social relations, attempt to restore a sense of community destroyed by capitalism. But, of course, such an attempt is always in the interests of the captains of industry—by participating in modern, media-based culture we implicate ourselves even more deeply in inauthentic, unfulfilling social relations.

The cultural criticism of the Frankfurt School most clearly limns the dangers of lost community in relation to media influence.[4] As émigrés to America during the 1930s, scholars such as Adorno, Horkheimer, Lowenthal, and Marcuse brought fears of totalitarianism to their analyses of the relationships between mass culture and mass society. The American inflection on their thought is to focus on issues of meaning rather than of power, on issues of experience rather than of expression. Nonetheless, the specter of totalitarian rule implicit in the work of the Frankfurt School still haunts the mass society thesis in America and shadows much of the criticism of mass culture.[5]

In mass society theory's positing of modern social relations as atomized, we get an image of modern man cut loose from traditional bonds, adrift in a dangerous sea, awash in falseness he cannot discern because he has no stable guides to truth. In short, we get *the image of the estranged, vulnerable media audience, awash in illusion and triviality.* Traditional, communal life offers individuals stable and sustaining meanings, while mass society offers only contradictory, fluctuating, and false images.

If we substitute Macdonald's "art" or Boorstin's "facts" for the words "communal life," and "mass media" for "mass society," in the sentence above, we find the basic claims of their media criticism: Art and facts (tradition) offer individuals stable and sustaining meanings, while the media (mass society) offer only contradictory, fluctuating, and false images.

In this reading, the media are extensions of mass society; they penetrate vulnerable individual consciousness with their specious replacements for lost organic unity. Both identity and connection are put at risk by modernity, the mass society perspective argues; the media further destabilize identity and connection, the media critique maintains.

Just as the mass society discourse contrasts tradition with modernity, the mass culture critique pits more ideal forms of communication, like "art" and "information," against the mass media. Stable and reliable meanings (supposedly once available) are now displaced and deformed. Individuals become vulnerable to the cheap and shallow appeals of totalitarianism and/or modernity, because they no longer have access to the strength and solace available in community and/or traditional cultural forms. The underlying charge is that society/mass media separate and isolate us from each other and from the moral and ethical standards that once guided us, and could now, perhaps, save us from ourselves.

Authority/Power

In an ideal American democracy, authority resides in a figurative public, with the power to implement policy through a representative government. In European practice, traditional authority was more tangible—rulers held power via lineage and law, were in control in ways that were more concrete and visible. The loss of such traditional lines of authority made the prospect of mass society, with an aimless, rootless mass vulnerable to despotism, a frightening but likely prospect.

In America, the lack of traditional lines of authority could be seen as liberating, as "natural." Freedom from the "constraints" of traditional authority would allow the will of the people, protected by government, codified in law, to wield legitimate power finally and freely.

What becomes frightening in American mass society theory is not, initially, a fear of fascist dictatorship, but instead a fear of a crude and crass public, one that displays no "natural" aristocratic tendencies. In giving power to the people, American thought must rely on the ability of "the people" to make wise and just decisions. If all men are created equal and have equal access to "truth" in the open marketplace of ideas, then a natural aristocracy should emerge, as particular individuals become recognized as statesmen, supported by the will of the people.

A mob, on the other hand, is a manipulated, irrational public. A mob does not cherish or protect self-government. It is made up of uneducated, emotional, uncultivated people. They prove the need, in a mass democracy, to seek and maintain reliable ways to form just and humane public opinion, if rational discussion in community is no longer available.

As social theory develops in twentieth-century America, it becomes increasingly concerned with problems of "the public" and "public opinion." Earlier notions of democracy must be reworked to accommodate the new kinds of social relations that are emerging. Yet the originating egalitarian impulses cannot be denied or ignored—"the people," at least in the abstract, must be seen as capable of wise, humane, and just self-rule.

Yet, to the critics, "the people" seem unworthy of the power that has been given to them. They seem, instead, to be capable of irrational, emotional, moblike responses. Why? Is American faith in the public misplaced? Could the founding principles of democratic life be fairy tales?

With the mass society theory, the answer to these troubling questions lies in the alienation and atomization resulting from "shattered" traditional bonds. Modernity, not "the people," is to blame. In the mass media critique, the answer lies in the evil influences of mass communication. As, for example, Boorstin (1972) and Postman (1985) tell it, the media, not "the people," are to blame.

Unresolved aspects of the power/authority unit idea can help to explain the vehemence with which the media are attacked. In the mass society argument, power is vested in organized institutions that penetrate a passive, vulnerable mass. When the media (as institutions of mass society) are deemed to be powerful, their power is ascribed to them in relation to the fears that the public is increasingly powerless.

The media receive the full brunt of fears about how power/authority operates in mass society. The media are deemed responsible for whatever is seen as wrong with the modern democratic process. If the public is apathetic, it is because they have become passive in the face of mass mediation. If the public is capricious, it is because the media offer them illusions, not real information. If the public is boorish, it is because the media have made them so, by offering them trash instead of art.

In American social theory, the public *must* be active, wise, and educated for modern democracy to succeed. Yet "the public" does not always act in the ways that social critics deem appropriate, and blame must be found somewhere. The media, because they are pervasive, commercial, and politically implicated, are the available scapegoats. *Seen as alien forces imposed on society, the mass media, rather than the innate traits of "the people," can be condemned.* Transformational power is ascribed to the media, a power so great that it can subvert the natural democratic processes that would otherwise emerge. Hidden in the claims of media power are deeper fears about the very possibility of modern democracy.

It is mostly in connection to the maintenance of public power that concerns about news media become articulated. What becomes obvious to observers as diverse as Dewey, Lippmann, and Mills is that the news media do not offer the kind of information best suited to the protection of public wisdom, and thus reliable public power.

To Dewey (1927/1947), news does not offer the kind of information that will spark discussion, that will connect people in vivid, conversational community. For Lippmann (1922), the media offer inadequate, faulty pictures of reality; they foster a public opinion based on illusion. Lippmann's concerns prefigure Boorstin's. For Mills (1956), the media are centralized and impersonal, part of a power elite that further distances the public from the true sources of power, and they invade and deflect the public's ability to recognize and act in their own democratic interests.[6]

Mills's critique contains much of what continues to trouble commentators about the mass media. If modern society is indeed mass, if we are less and less connected to each other or to traditional modes of belief, we are more likely to believe what is told to us by those "in the know," less likely to think for ourselves or question authority. "The community of publics" initially dreamed of in America is becoming more and more a "society of masses," and thus more open to penetration by the media.

Because American social thought sees ideal power as residing in a generalized public, operationalized as public opinion and actualized in voting, it becomes concerned about "modern" public opinion being formed by the mass media, an untrustworthy, self-serving source. If the media control public opinion, then we are at the mercy of a radical, conservative, or commercial entity, depending on the critic's point of view.[7]

The American media operate in self-interested ways—they will present those images most likely to attract an audience and thus to make money. They also are self-serving, conservative critics argue; they report only news critical to the administration, with which they have an adversarial relationship. Radical critics argue the opposite, that the news media disseminate only those opinions that maintain and serve the status quo. In either case, the issue is the power of media accounts to substitute for reality. The fear is that their accounting of the world will not provide the appropriate basis for sound public opinion.

The modern "crisis of authority" is perceived in relation to a loss of democratic community, but is discussed in relation to media influence. Perceiving of the media as powerful, as molders of public opinion, raises the specter of a pseudodemocratic state, where the public assumes that it is informed but in fact is being manipulated. Thus, as Postman sees it, we mistake truncated and entertaining happy news for information; from Boorstin's view, we mistake pseudo-events for reality. We trust forms of communication that systematically distort our necessary knowledge of the world.

We see, then, that expectations of the mass media are in direct relation to concerns about the possibility of political democracy in a modern society. To the extent that the news media are seen as offering inadequate, biased, or reactionary information, they are criticized. This critique easily extends to entertainment and advertising, as other ways that the public gains knowledge about the world. Good, accurate, reliable knowledge is seen as protecting the public from manipulation, and thus protecting the public's ability to participate fully in self-government.

If the public does not have reliable knowledge via the media, if it becomes misinformed, lulled into complacency, stuffed full of half-truths, it will cease to function as a democratic public, will sink into the sullen anomie of the mass, and then (incorporating mass society fears) will become vulnerable to totalitarian rule. In this construction, the media become the safeguard of democracy, and yet the media do not, in the eyes of most critics, adequately fulfill their appointed role.

It is in this way that media power becomes viewed as insidious. It divests the public of its rightful authority, but it does so in ways that appear (paradoxically) to confer authority. The news media are poseurs, to most critics, masquerading as being in the public interest. They claim to be offering neutral information on which to base public action, but in actuality they are commercial, value-laden, self-interested enterprises.

The venom in attacks on the modern press can be related to this deeper conceptualization of American power residing in the public, a public that is being cheated of its rightful position of authority. The media have come to replace the public, to "mediate" between politicians and the people, and their power is seen as unnatural and self-serving.

Class/Status

In European thought, concern with the proper role of the elite, with how the best thought, leadership, and culture can be maintained, with how to prevent or deflect mob rule, is less problematic than it is in American thought. In America, such concerns struggle with the label "elitist," because whatever is worthy can and should already exist in a robust, democratic populace. Yet, as we have seen, there is fear that the tastes of the masses are not trustworthy. The seeming "low quality" of the most popular media content seems to be evidence of this untrustworthiness, although blame is only uneasily, and thus relatively rarely, placed on any inherent "vulgarity" in the masses.

The issue of status in America is a prominent fault line. In a democratic, egalitarian society, it is unclear how status is to be assigned, or how (or if) critical standards are to be located and maintained. The media become the battleground for status ascription, condemned for the quality of their content, for their presentation of celebrities as heroes, for their indiscriminate promotion of products, ideas, values. This condemnation allows an elision of a direct attack on the audience.[8]

The mass culture debate, as we have seen in Macdonald (1962), engages the connections among aesthetic taste, class, and status. Standards of evaluation are sought that are somehow naturally "true" rather than uncomfortably related to exigencies of wealth or status. Essential standards are sought, standards that will "speak" to the "natural good taste" of the democratically cultivated American.[9] Such a search is chimerical, but in American cultural thought it is chronic, at least until the mid-twentieth century.[10]

In everyday life, however, culture continues to be presented and received in relation to aesthetic standards that mask status ascription only incompletely. Those cultural forms that are enjoyed by the well educated and wealthy are almost always deemed more worthy than those enjoyed by the uneducated and poor. These social (ultimately political) ascriptions can be disguised as aesthetic differences in "difficulty" or "insight" or "complexity."[11]

In American social thought, the desire to celebrate modern society as open, egalitarian, and democratic is undercut by the evaluation of cultural content as more and less worthy, and a related belief that "raising" the content will cultivate the appropriate sensibilities in a democratic public. *A cultivation metaphor becomes the way to call for standards without sounding like an elitist*—one can ask for "better" media as a representative of "the people," who would be aesthetically and morally improved if only they had the appropriate content in which to share.

This becomes the American way out of the mass culture debate, a way that does not criticize the innate sensibilities of the public, but instead criticizes the quality of the product and the producers. If only the media would create and disseminate a higher quality of cultural material, the critic implies, the people would learn to love it, and would become somehow "better" themselves.

The snobbishness of the assumption that "better" is whatever the critic prefers, which has been institutionally legitimated by the privileged and incorporated into an unreflexive canon of "the best," is for the most part ignored. Instead, the call for "quality" cultural content appears to be a populist call for improvement, in the name of the innate, as-yet-undeveloped, "good taste" of "the people."

Sacred/Secular

I have suggested that a characteristic of the media/modernity narrative is a theme of pollution or contamination. Another term for this would be desecration—the making profane of the previously sacred. This religious imagery is not, I believe, arbitrary or accidental. As Nisbet (1966) suggests in his sacred/secular opposition, the modern age is a secular one in which "the sacred" has been circumscribed and religion separated from the state. This is, of course, particularly true in American public life, where the separation of church and state is axiomatic, if still at issue.

Yet constitutional doctrine does not prevent the blurring of distinctions, and, as we find in much of everyday life, a sanctification of spheres. This sanctification allows particular aspects of life to be deemed redemptive. As will be discussed in Chapter 3, art, information, and education, if they are "pure," are believed to have the ability to resacralize the profane.

The vehemence, rather than simply the nature, of the attacks on the mass media can be explained by this modern expectation of secular redemption. Modern, and American, faith in the possibility of sacred transformation underlies the expectations placed on mass communication. To the extent that the media are seen as embodying or influencing or displacing "better" cultural forms, they are charged with the redemptive possibilities ascribed to those forms. As will be discussed in detail in Chapter 3, when the media fail to redeem us—as public art, or information, or education, or technology—there is disappointment, anger, and blame.

The logic of the discourse goes something like this: If art can transform American life into a humane society of letters, and us into a lively, engaged public, then so could the media, if only they disseminated art. We are not a lively, engaged public, and the media do not carry real art, and thus the media can be blamed for failing to transform us, as they so easily could. Instead of offering us access to transcendence, the media smother us with rubbish.

If information can allow the public to make wise decisions, then so could the media, if they offered the kind of information needed to help us understand and make good choices in the modern world. But instead of offering us access to real knowledge, they give us simplistic, one-sided accounts and news turned into entertainment. They prevent the transcendence that information can offer.

If education is seen as eliminating ignorance, as offering wisdom and truth to everyone, then the media as mass educators could inform and enlighten all who participate in them. Yet ignorance is still rampant; wisdom, truth, and enlightenment do not reign, and again the media can be blamed. They do not offer "real" knowledge, the right kind; instead, they offer lies and falsehoods that even displace the education children receive in school. They prevent the transcendence education could offer.

Sacred powers attributed to art, information, and education are combined in a characteristically American faith in technology. If technology can liberate us from the bonds of nature, can give us mastery and control over the irrational, and if electronic technology can redeem us from the evils of the machine age, then surely the new mass media will bring about a new global village, a communal utopia. The old media technologies did not offer us transcendence, but the new media technologies might.

The media critique, as we have seen, always avoids a direct attack on "the people." Tremendous secular power must be ascribed to the mass media if a faith in the natural goodness of the people is to be maintained. If the critics believe that people are everywhere foolish and irrational, that prejudice and ignorance are rampant, then blame can be placed on the media, which deflect and deform the people's innate ability to be rational, accepting, wise. The evils of modern life exist because the media offer a deformed vision that prevents the people from finding ways to live together well. Thus the supposed power of art, information, education, technology, and the "natural" abilities of a democratic people to build an ideal society have been subverted. To the extent that the media can be seen as potentially sacred, and therefore transcendent, the media can be blamed for their failure to redeem.

The promises of modern American life, based on expectations of imminent transformation, by the media or by related forces of "progress," have not been met. The media are defined as bad art, as inadequate information, as evil educators, as dangerous technologies, and as a bad social influence, in order to explain why longed for social progress has not yet happened.

The vehemence of the media attack must be understood, then, in relation to this American expectation of social transformation. One aspect of this expectation is its religious imagery—the possibility of redemption. The modern age may well be secular, but it still has faith.

Alienation/Progress

The overriding faith of the modern age has been in progress. Yet "progress" no longer has its nineteenth-century ring of beneficence. Nisbet's last unit idea, alienation/progress, is the most problematic, since the terms are not really antonyms, and they do not directly refer to a tradition/modernity split.

Yet the dyad invokes the crucial contradiction of the modernity critique. *Progress* is a vague and general term implying betterment, improvement, an upward curve of benefits. *Alienation* is a vaguely scientific description of a modern existence, separated, isolated, and anxious. The central unanswered question in the discourse of modernity is, Does progress require alienation? What has never been fully worked out, in considerations of historical change, is whether the price of social progress must always be personal alienation.

Both progress and alienation, in American social thought, require the notion of individualism. Faith in the power of the individual to solve problems, invent machines, climb the social ladder, become wealthy, is a deeply American faith. But the same individual who can "progress" can also feel "alienated," cut off from the sustaining power of family, community, and religion. The haunting duality of material success at the expense of spiritual growth is embedded in the alienation/progress dyad.

Alienation is seen, by mass society critics, as the key psychological and social characteristic of the modern age. It defines the difference between community and society, and describes the sense of being isolated and alone in a crowded, fragmented life. Alienation is the dark twin of progress; it is the consequence of the uprooting that is modern change.

Progress, once a unidimensional positive attribute, has become ambiguous in the twentieth century. Progress has its price, and the price is seen as increasingly unpleasant. Not only alienation, but stress, suicide, broken homes, violent crimes, homelessness, environmental destruction—all are by-products of progress, and all have been copiously documented and discussed.

Progress, like modernity, is Janus-faced—it is both the wondrous possibility and the terrifying prospect of "the new." Like the relationship between city and country, "the new" can be exciting, diverse, multiple, and fast paced, or it can be debilitating, stressful, exhausting, and overwhelming. "The old" can be boring, stagnant, and claustrophobic or peaceful, secure, and familiar. We can ascribe to contemporary life, in comparison with an imagined past, all things wonderful or all things terrible.

Yet in both positive and negative readings of modernity, an increasing pace, multiplicity, and engagement are seen as characteristic. Such characterizations can be used to celebrate or bemoan the quality of contemporary experience. Since the late nineteenth century, most critics bemoan the influence of modernity on the quality of individual experience.

Neurasthenia is a disease ascribed to the hectic pace of late nineteenth-century life. The history of spas and rest cures attests to a widespread belief in the healing powers of escape from the enervating tensions of "modern" nineteenth-century life, especially for delicate, upper-class women. Alienation, with its origins in Marx's analysis of industrialization, becomes combined with an American emphasis on the need to recover energy and spontaneity in contemporary experience.

More recent critics continue the argument that progress has resulted in overstimulation and fragmentation and, ultimately, a kind of helpless and hopeless exhaustion. For Klapp (1986), we live in a time where we are overloaded with stimuli but emptied of meaning; for Lifton (1968), we are protean, struggling to synthesize identity fragments into a coherent self in a world with far too many choices.

The "anomie" that characterizes alienation is the result, we now say, of the "stress" of modern life. Rather than neurasthenia, we now diagnose "workaholism," and prescribe relaxation and rest. Notice how anomie is also seen as the characteristic state of the heavy TV viewer, "conditioned" by exposure to the tube. The "addicted" viewer is defined as passive, paranoid, isolated, overstimulated, and unable to reflect or think logically.

In the ambivalence about progress, in the fears about alienation, we hear again the themes of community/society, concerns with issues of identity, connection, power, and meaning. These concerns are laid at the doorstep of both modernity and the mass media.

What we are seeing is how *the media are a terrain in which concerns about modern life are played out*. The media become an inkblot into which are read the problematic issues of modernity. The mass media are seen as *bearers* of modernity, in that they deepen and extend the disintegrative aspects of mass society. They are also seen as *deflectors* of modernity, in that they prevent or divert the liberating and redemptive aspects of mass society. In either case, the media serve as *touchstones* of modernity; they offer an arena of criticism that includes the key tensions of the modernity critique, without ever directly confronting or resolving them.

Media/Modernity as Inauthentic Other

The media are seen as alien forms, imposed on society from the outside. Their invention, adoption, and use are conceived of as unnatural intrusions into separate, ongoing American social, political, and cultural life. As outside forces, the media can spoil and pervert what already exists, and deflect and deform what would otherwise naturally develop.

Modernity, too, is deemed "unnatural," in that its emergence is seen as destroying more authentic, traditional habits, practices, and forms of society. Modernity, as industrialization and urbanization, is predominantly conceptualized as going against the natural rhythms of "traditional" man. But modernity, as "progress," is seen as inexorable; the tide of history is away from nature, toward civilization. Thus a key component of the theory of modernity, and a way to resolve the tensions between alienation and progress, has to do with what is deemed "natural" or "authentic."

"Authenticity" directly references beliefs about the relationships between the modern individual and modern society. The argument goes something like this: Tradition is "natural," and yet so is progress, but we have somehow ended up alienated; but since alienation is "unnatural," the wrong turn must have had something to do with our losing touch with the genuine, natural, deepest impulses of humanity. Thus the "natural" or the "authentic" can resolve the logical contradictions between tradition and progress.

As a concept, "authenticity" implies "naturalness"; it is what is best, most basic and true and real, in humankind's possibilities. It is what is lost in material progress and what is available in spiritual growth. So "authenticity" must be salvaged if "progress" is to be truly progressive. If the ills of modernity are to be mitigated, if modernity is to be truly progressive, then the "authentic" must be recognized and celebrated.

The problem of authenticity underlies Lears's (1981) analysis of turn-of-the-century antimodernist practices among northern-educated bourgeoisie. Lears argues that late nineteenth-century modern life was taken to be artificial and overcivilized, characterized by an "evasive banality." The response to this "inauthenticity" was a quest for vivid, rich, "authentic" experience through arts and crafts, medievalism, orientalism, and mind cures.[12]

The evidence Lears accumulates persuasively suggests that turn-of-the-century Americans defined society as a separate, distinct force. The workings of society could deleteriously affect the vulnerable, truth-seeking individual. Quests for authentic experience are individually mounted, against the grain of a society perceived as increasingly alien and inauthentic.

Congruently, Berman (1970) argues that authenticity becomes a self-conscious problem for modern man. Those who seek authenticity have come to see the world as one that "re-presses, alienates, divides, denies, destroys the self" (p. xvi). The search for authenticity "begins with an insistence that the social and political structures men live in are keeping the self stifled, chained down, locked up" (p. xix). What Berman calls the "politics of authenticity" is "a dream of an ideal community in which individuality will not be subsumed and sacrificed, but fully developed and expressed" (p. ix).

Such a politics, then, assumes a deep, true self that is di-verted, distorted, alienated, or suppressed by modern society. This self is most "authentic" when actively and creatively en-gaged in self-expression, a romantic impulse that Berman be-lieves is a deeply felt response to modernity. In the politics of authenticity, an alternative society is envisioned, one that is "fully modern" in that it imagines engaged, expansive, fluid expression for a collectivity of individuals.

"Authenticity" as a construct bears the weight of democratic dreams of an open, democratic society, where individuals cre-atively, spontaneously, and freely express their deepest, most natural feelings. In this vernacular theory of progressive tradi-tion/traditional progress, participation in "authentic" expres-sion allows transcendence of whatever is repressive in mod-ern society. Participation in the inauthentic expressions of the media, however, further enslaves the already stifled individual.

Locating the mass media as "inauthentic other" supports a demonology where blame for all social and cultural ills can be placed on the media alone. Viewing the media as an invasive, inauthentic, and destructive intruder, rather than as a contem-porary social and cultural practice, allows blame to be located and circumscribed.

It also allows the unresolved tensions of modernity—be-tween the loss of community and the promises of society, be-tween the loss of aristocratic authority and the possibilities of democratic power, between the dissolution of class and the reworkings of status, between the decline of the sacred and the rise of the secular—to be papered over. Progress would *not* be alienating, would be liberating and restorative, if only the media were somehow different. The best of tradition, its "authenticity," would prevail in modern, American progress.

Characterizing the media as an alien, unnatural intruder also allows a characteristically American hope—that there is an administrative solution to the problems of modernity. There is, in American thought, a belief that if the media can be "improved" (through legislative changes, or technological advancement, or public action), then the expected virtues of American life will finally flourish. Once blame has been located and circumscribed, reform is a straightforward process. Find the cause and the cure is assured—media reform then becomes a safe and easy way to transform society.

Media reform becomes seen as a way both to neutralize an evil force and to liberate a redemptive one. If the "right" kinds of media are created, then the "right" kind of modern life will flourish. Such a faith invigorates media criticism, but avoids acknowledgment and resolution of the dualities described above. What are the "right" kinds of media? The "right" kind of modern life? And can changing the media really change the world?

Polluting the Future

The above discussion has shown how the media, as representation of modernity, have been seen as "unnatural others" that somehow pollute and defile everyday life. But the media can also be seen as polluting, by deflection, a desired future. The media can also be seen as somehow preventing a "natural course" of modernity—progress toward utopia.

This second vision of the media—as a deflection of progress—is a complex one. It engages beliefs about the nature and promise of social change, as well as about technology, corporate capitalism, and democracy. It locates the media as somehow preventing a "natural" outcome. In this way, the media are seen as "polluting the future."

The assumption is that the media *could* have fostered an ideal, utopian society, but (for some reason) they have not yet fulfilled their potential. They have sold out, have become part of the problem, have failed to offer the solution they once promised. This aspect of media criticism views modernity as ever advancing. This view directly contrasts with the belief that modernity degrades all that was once "pure" in premodern life. In this more pessimistic view, modernity is decadence and history is decay—what was wholesome and authentic in past civilizations has become, in our own time, corrupt and corrupting. In the pessimistic view dominant among social critics, the media are bearers of corruption, and thus bearers of modernity.

But the story of civilization has also been told very differently. Modernity has also been narrativized as a story of progressive, even triumphant achievement. How are the media understood in this optimistic view of the past, present, and future?

Interestingly, in this cheerful perspective on modern life, the media do *not* become defined as valued bearers of upbeat modernity. Hypothetically, the mass media could be viewed as technological triumphs, bringing the fruits of modern progress to the populace. *Yet even in the positive reading of modernity, current media influence is deplored.* The contemporary mass media are still defined as corrupt, corrupting, polluting, defiling. Only the imaginary "media of the future" are viewed positively. And these new media are allocated tremendous redemptive powers.

The double-edged modernity narrative—as decadent finale or desirable prelude—is a fundamental fault line in American social thought. It underlies the tensions, raised but not resolved, in American social criticism, and it inevitably spills over into assumptions about the role and influence of media in society. This shows, again, how social narratives need not be univocal, or logical, or coherent, to have cultural power. Beliefs about the decline of civilization can coexist with beliefs about civilization's advance. Each vision, although conflicting, can be drawn upon by individuals or groups, at different times, in different ways, for different purposes.

But in either case, the present is never neutral. Current conditions are always understood in relation to an interpreted past and an imagined future. This means that beliefs about contemporary life, if examined, tell us which versions of the past and future are being adopted. We can recognize how particular narratives are being used to represent and justify interpretations of the present. For example, when modernity is equated with improving conditions, with cultural, social, political, and economic advance, then the past is understood to be an inadequate prelude. The past is seen as a misguided rough draft to the present, which is opening onto a triumphant future. Efforts to collect, store, study, or revere the past (a humanities tradition) are seen as far less interesting and valuable than efforts to manifest and promote the future (via, usually, the social and physical sciences).

The positive, booster version of modernity thus defines contemporary life as an arena of scientific discovery that makes possible an extraordinarily desirable future. The present is seen as an exciting time of mysterious technological breakthroughs. Particular individuals—scientists and engineers—are hailed as holding the "keys to the future." Particular systems—industrial and corporate—are celebrated as "making the future now." The present becomes defined as a laboratory out of which will come, swiftly and magically, an ideal future.

The World of Tomorrow

This utopian narrative of the "World of Tomorrow" develops most fully in American life in the early to mid-twentieth century. We find it celebrated in the various world's fairs and

Disney theme parks, and circulated in popular science magazines, industry pamphlets, educational films, and grade school newsletters. The World of Tomorrow offers a vision of technological advance that occurs naturally, as science marches on, discovering new and exciting alternatives to all that has previously bedeviled us.

This is a world of consumer-citizens eagerly participating in a technological garden of delights. It is a world of abundance, of leisure, of camaraderie, and of ease. The nuclear family remains intact, selecting products and pastimes from a cornucopia of new inventions. Work is engaging and rewarding, and there is plenty of time to relax and enjoy life. No one is overly rich or overly poor—everyone seems to share in the imagined largess of the new era.

In this imagined future, there are neighborhoods that combine the relaxed intimacy of rural life with the vibrant delight of urban areas, and there is health care that is miraculously restorative and available to all who need it. In short, because of "progress," all the perceived hardships of past and present life have disappeared.

A key component of the World of Tomorrow is the elimination of pain and frustration. Physical and mental illness, the indignities of aging, and the cruelty of handicaps have virtually disappeared. Inefficiency, a perceived cause of frustration, is also a thing of the past. In this streamlined, expertly designed world, everything runs smoothly, easily, and efficiently. Transportation is quick and convenient, food purchase and preparation are quick and convenient, communication is quick and convenient. The true potential of modernity—to minimize hardships and maximize pleasure—has finally been realized.

The World of Tomorrow is a friendly, relaxed mass society, where consumer-citizens gratefully share in the bounty made possible by technological advance. They may not understand exactly how their heliports, or telescreens, or food-o-laters work, but they are pleased by the result—an abundant, leisure-filled, pain-free life. They are the "audience" for the show put on by the new elite, specialists in science and technology who devise and implement the products that progress makes possible.[13]

This vision can seem, today, both engagingly naive and suspiciously totalitarian. The dronelike gratitude of the masses, the exalted expertise of the technicians, and the streamlined efficiency can signify to us a dystopic vision of the future. Today we are heirs to the duality of the modernity discourse, especially in relation to a technological utopia. We have become familiar with the demonic undercurrents of the technological vision. We have become conversant with a more pessimistic discourse available in books, movies, magazine articles, and television shows.

This dystopian possibility was recognized, in the early twentieth century, in the writings of a number of social critics and intellectuals.[14] Drawing on the dark side of the hopes and fears that had earlier accompanied the Industrial Revolution, these writers described a frightening outcome of technological advance. Their twentieth-century "world of tomorrow" was mechanistic, inhumane, a robotlike enslavement to the demands of an impersonal, bureaucratic society.

Dystopic versions of a technological future can be found in Orwell's *1984*, Huxley's *Brave New World*, Lang's *Metropolis*, and Chaplin's *Modern Times*. Later, they move into the popular discourse via concerns with nuclear holocaust, invasions by extraterrestrials, and visions of environmental disaster. By the 1970s, the "rhetoric of the technological sublime" had been challenged in both intellectual and popular accounts of the future.

It appears as if declining faith in the future begins with cultural critics who interpret technology as antithetical to human values. Drawing on images already developing in nineteenth-century responses to "the machine in the garden"[15] they describe a world where all that makes life pungent, idiosyncratic, and engaging has been extirpated, replaced by something bland, homogenized, and dull. The result of technological "advance" is a life of bovine contentment that is actually en-slavement.

Postman (1985) is an example of a critic who makes direct connections between media criticism and dystopic visions of the future. By claiming that Huxley was "more right" than Orwell in his fears for the future, Postman allies himself with the dystopian critics. And by conflating media influence with modernity, he represents a longer tradition of conflation, where ascribed media influences are taken to parallel the assumed characteristics of modernity.

Ideals may be most vociferously defended when they are perceived as being most under siege. Douglas (1977) calls this "the sentimental lie," where what is actually being eroded is vehemently (and romantically) defended in public rhetoric. As evidence accumulated that technological developments did *not* automatically ameliorate social evils, that they could even in-crease pain and hardship, could "turn on us" in the form of nuclear holocaust or environmental disaster, the defense of the vision of technological redemption became even stronger. That the height of American displays of technocratic faith oc-curred between World Wars I and II, when the devastating influences of technological warfare, and economic recession, were obvious, supports this notion.

The World's Fairs of 1933 and 1939 celebrated an ideal world that transcended war and poverty, just as Disneyland and the Epcot Center celebrated, in the 1950s and 1980s, a world with-out political strife, environmental pollution, or nuclear mis-siles. To visit these public arenas of technocratic celebration is to recognize, and to participate in, the tenacity of the rheto-ric of the World of Tomorrow, even in an era of supposed disenchantment.

Unameliorated futuristic despair is not widespread, in spite of the gloomy critiques of modernity circulated in intellectual and scholarly circles. The pessimistic outlook seems, particu-larly for college students, to be something of a veneer. Just below the surface is a faith in future possibility, in ways out of disaster, if not permanently, at least for a while. Class discussions that begin with cynical claims about the prospects of civilization often become extraordinary testaments to faith in the future of humankind, especially through unexamined, but recurrent, expressions of faith in the powers of "information" and "technology."

These testaments suggest the influence of the boomlet of newspaper and magazine articles, appearing in the 1970s, that heralded the dawning Information Age.[16] These are concrete examples of the technocratic utopian rhetoric developing throughout the twentieth century. Their claim is that, in a technologically advanced future society, communication will be salvational—the new media will bring about the previously deflected (but now still achievable) World of Tomorrow.

Media as New Technologies

This faith in the redemptive potential of new media technologies is nothing new—it characterizes the history of each new communication form. From the early newspapers to the telegraph, telephone, typewriter, radio, film, television, satellites, home computers, cable technology, and fiber optics, each new form has been greeted with extravagant hopes. Always, there are fears and doubts, too, but the overriding impulse, in American social thought, has been to celebrate the new communication technology as redeeming a particular vision of an ideal America.[17]

Carey and Quirk discuss faith in the redemptive power of communication technology in relation to "the rhetoric of the electrical sublime."[18] They argue that faith in electrical power, including the new electronic media, adopted the language, and the contradictions, inherent in an earlier American faith in mechanical energy. The mythos of the electronic revolution celebrates, as does its predecessor, an about-to-arrive future of social harmony, community, abundance, and beneficence.

The rhetoric of the electronic sublime depends on this very American faith in a new middle way, between primal nature and repressive civilization, and on a view of the future as a both human-made and naturally evolving zone of perfectibility. This heritage thus *doubly* endows the new communications media—they inherit an American faith in the redemptive powers of culture *and* of technology, and thus of the possibility of a perfected American future. Such a dream of redemption is the shadow against which the new media are evaluated, and in relation to which they inevitably disappoint.

Davis (1976) examines the popular discourse surrounding the development of film, radio, and television. In an exhaustive survey of commentary found in popular magazines from 1891 to 1955, he identifies a number of lines of argument that appeared with each new medium. His work offers evidence of how new media have been heir to American expectations of transformation.

His analysis shows how the advent of film and broadcasting sparked a dual response, an advocacy and an attack, that incorporated a tension between hopes of felicity and fears of destruction. Advocates argued that the new medium could correct past weaknesses and provide new ways to achieve an ideal America. Critics argued that the new media destroy traditional values, weakening and eroding standards, goals, and ideals. Where advocates see church, family, education, and politics being strengthened and revivified, attackers see those institutions as being eclipsed, even replaced by the corrupt new media.

The advent of each new form sparks a period of prediction, Davis finds, in which the two perspectives prophesy very different futures. This is followed by a period of evaluation in which the two perspectives evaluate contemporary conditions less dramatically, but still differently. Before media celebrants can become disheartened by the nonutopian character of contemporary life, a new communication form develops, one that is predicted once again to make possible a communal, harmonious, egalitarian future.

This is the interpretive heritage being mobilized in response to today's new communication technologies, the so-called revolutions in cable and computing. The Information Age was expected to dawn finally, fully, once cable television became widespread and home computers became linked to each other and to vast information banks. As before, this new age would be decentralized, harmonious, educated, communal, and, of course, even more "democratic," making possible the perfect future that is always waiting for us, just over the horizon.

Media as Technological Progress

That Americans believe in the likelihood of utopia, and that they define technology as equivalent to progress, is noted by Segal (1985). Technology *embodies* progress in American social thought, rather than being seen as a means to achieve desired political, economic, social, and cultural changes.

Technology, in American utopian thought, is allied with terms like *evolution, equilibrium, efficiency, system, organization, planning,* and *rationalization,* he notes. These terms offer a late nineteenth-century bureaucratic blending of organicism and mechanization.[19] They represent yet another attempt to resolve the inherent contradictions between the American dreams of the sublime and the American dreams of power. They are another way to dissolve difference by invoking an outside force.

What underlies the response to the mass media as new technologies is a heritage of technological utopianism that endows technology with transformative power and envisions a redemptive American future. This is what supports a faith, in American thought, in the possibility of a technological cure. Technology is invoked as a force that automatically dissolves conflict and offers harmony. When the media are defined as a technology, they become heir to an overdetermined metaphor. The full burden of American expectations of technology is then placed on the mass media.

So, under a metaphor of "media as technology," the media are a site for social commentary, but in a way that obscures the complexities of that heritage. By treating new media technologies as potentially redemptive, we are simply "waiting to be saved." Through some longed-for influence of mysterious technological forces, all that is irksome, evil, and unfair will be washed away, and an ideal new world will emerge and flourish.

Notice how, for optimist and pessimist alike, technological transformation is both "natural" and "human-made"—it occurs through the immanent powers of the technological forms themselves, but also through the conscious construction of those technologies by the expertise, the applied science, of modern man. Distinction between a natural sublime and a conscious power is collapsed in the ethos of technological transformation.

In a serial fashion, each new form that appears is expected to overcome or exacerbate the failings of the old. Cable and computer technologies are only the most recent in a long line of communication forms, including the telegraph, typewriter, film, radio, and television, to elicit a chorus of prophetic language. The same dreams (of harmony, balance, community, equality, and participation) and the same nightmares (of discord, destruction, fragmentation, stratification, and alienation) are dreamed each time.

What is inevitably elided in this recurring pattern are the deeper questions about human nature, the social order, the relationships among culture, society, and power, and the constructedness of past, present, and future. These are complex issues and relationships, yet they must be engaged if we are to understand, evaluate, and refigure the relationships among media, culture, and society. When we make claims about media influence, for whatever purposes, we are making claims about how the human world has been, is now, and can be.

It is important to recognize and examine the assumptions we use when we discuss our common modern life. By doing so, we make more likely the development of inclusive public languages, of more various and representative ways to interpret the past and the future in relation to the present. We can, once we recognize some of the terms in which we think, more directly engage contradictions, recognize incommensurable differences, and acknowledge the unfair, the vicious, and the cruel consequences, as well as the liberating, respectful, and kind consequences, of particular actions, systems, and choices.

Media discourse, fully located in relation to the discourse of modernity, offers us an arena for this process of recognition, clarification, engagement, and acknowledgment. Because the media spark such widespread discussion, because they already serve as a touchstone for ambivalence about the modern condition, we can use assumptions about media influence to foster discussions about contemporary life.

But to make such discussion useful, we must first acknowledge just what it is we are mobilizing in our claims. We must recognize and examine the premises of our discussion. So far, media criticism has been characterized here by the work of four specific critics, through description of their basic claims and brief consideration of their premises. The criticism of modernity was then addressed to demonstrate how it parallels and intersects with media commentary. The characteristic elements and unresolved contradictions in the media/modernity story have been highlighted, and it has been suggested how blaming the media tells a simplistic, reassuring story that avoids direct confrontation of the contradictions within it.

Notes

1. The critiques of postmodern society (Hassan, 1986; Jameson, 1984, among others) often extend claims previously made about modern society. Assumptions about the "before-time" continue, with pre/postmodern society seen as more linear or coherent, and evaluated either positively (as more authentic) or negatively (as more repressive) than postmodern society. For a clear contrast between these points of view, compare McRobbie (1986) and Merquior (1986).
2. Leon Bramson is one of the few American scholars who has addressed media, modernity, and American social thought simultaneously and criti-

cally. His book, *The Political Context of Sociology* (1961), is an all too infrequently read classic.

3. Bramson's interpretation of the concerns that shaped early mass communication research is less sympathetically developed in Stuart Hall's (1982) contention that American research was an attempt to prove that "pluralism works here." An intriguing analysis of how American mass communication research proceeds in relation to social and cultural purposes, both in its conduct and in its deployment for social policy, can be found in Rowland (1983).

4. See Martin Jay's work for an analytical overview of the ideas of these scholars, particularly *The Dialectical Imagination* (1973).

5. See, for example, the collection on media and mass culture edited by Lazere (1987), who says that "the contributors to this collection have assimilated Frankfurt School and other recent European, Latin American and British criticism, but most of them are Americans speaking in their native voice about their native culture" (p. xi).

6. These considerations of news are discussed in far more detail in Chapter 3, in the section headed "News as Modern Information."

7. That critics from very different political perspectives find the media to be representative of some dangerous "other" perspective suggests that news coverage is not as univocal, or monolithic, as they fear.

8. An illustration of the problem of status in American society is Gans's discussion of taste cultures in *Popular Culture and High Culture* (1974).

9. This is Walt Whitman's expectation in "Democratic Vistas" (1871/1959).

10. Herbert Croly (1909), Van Wyck Brooks (1915), Waldo Frank (1937), and Constance Rourke (1942) represent some of the critics who sought to recognize, define, and exhort into being an authentic, modern, but still worthy, American cultural tradition.

11. This can be demonstrated using an exercise I call the "art/trash game." Three categories are created—high, middle, low—and various cultural forms are considered, such as painting, novels, music, television shows, sports, newspapers, and magazines. When people are asked to list what "most people" would call high, middle, and low forms of each, each category is rapidly and jovially filled. Once the lists have been assembled, it is obvious that those forms that are old, European, institutionalized, patronized by the wealthy, and/or involve education tend to be deemed high culture, while those that are recent, local, uninstitutionalized, patronized by the poor, and do not involve education are deemed to be low culture. Thus we find Rembrandt versus black-velvet Elvises; Tolstoy versus Harlequin romances; Haydn versus heavy metal; British drama on PBS versus American afternoon soaps; polo versus bowling; the *New York Times* versus the *National Enquirer*; the *New Yorker* versus *People*. The "middle" category tends to represent middle-class, mass-mediated culture, for example: Norman Rockwell or art reproductions, Stephen King, Top 40 music, prime-time television, baseball, local newspapers, *Time* or *Newsweek*. Assumed aesthetic

differences in intrinsic merits are difficult to defend once the class/status underpinnings are demonstrated this clearly.

12. Interestingly, Lears (1981) argues that these individualistic, therapeutic responses, conceived of as alternatives to the inauthentic modern life, ultimately (and paradoxically) paved the way for twentieth-century consumer culture. Thus, unlike Ewen, Lears locates consumer practices as extensions of historically recognizable cultural and social practices of "the people."

13. The nature and contradictions of this vision of technological modernity are discussed in de Lauretis, Huyssen, and Woodward (1980), Goldberg and Strain (1987), Clarke (1979), Layton (1973), and Marquis (1986).

14. Lewis Mumford's work is especially interesting in this regard, as it begins with an analysis of past utopian visions and ends with an indictment of technocratic society. His struggle is to imagine (and thus make possible) a more humane American life, balancing spiritual and technological imperatives. His writings reveal an increasing pessimism about the possibilities of creating this balance. The best overview of Mumford's intellectual trajectory is *Interpretations and Forecasts* (1973).

15. This is Leo Marx's (1964) apt phrase, as is "the rhetoric of the technological sublime."

16. A good example in book form is Williams (1982).

17. This historical pattern of hopes and fears "from Morse to McLuhan" is well developed in Czitrom (1982), who draws on earlier work by Carey (now collected in *Communication as Culture*, 1989) on the telegraph, the Chicago school, and Innis and McLuhan.

18. This phrase reworks Leo Marx's; it, and the ideas in the following paragraphs, are developed in Carey and Quirk's "The Mythos of the Electronic Revolution" and "The History of the Future," which appear, somewhat revised, in Carey (1989).

19. This notion of an uneasy blending of organicism and mechanization in the late nineteenth century, seen as fragile but inexorable, is nicely developed in Wiebe's (1967) chapter "Revolution in Values."

3

Three Dominant Metaphors

If we are to find better ways to tell the story of media-in-society, we need to consider the full range of arguments that have been mobilized in media discourse. In this chapter we consider claims of media influence made not only by social and cultural critics, but also by academic researchers and popular writers.

Three contrasting images organize the discussion: media as art form, media as information source, and media as educational tool. These images are general, vague, and often overlapping, but they can be seen as informing, organizing, and underlying almost all discussion of media influence.

These three images are rarely commented on directly. Critics tend to employ each of them as a kind of master metaphor, organizing their arguments by implicit reference to the particular concerns of art, or information, or education in contemporary life. Each image seems to naturally evoke an associated pattern of claims, logic, and concerns about the influences of the mass media.

This implicit use of a master metaphor, as if the media were "obviously" to be understood as a form of art, or information, or education, obscures the consequences of such metaphorical deployment. To treat the mass media as a modern, commercial, industrial version of one of these three forms is to ensure the mobilization of a critique of corruption. *The media will appear to be decadent, inadequate, homogenized, or diluted versions of art, information, or education, when compared against an ideal formulation envisioned as flourishing in the past.*

The perceived absence of uplifting aesthetic expression, accurate information, and ennobling education in media content can easily be blamed on the influence of the media on society at large. Not only are the media devoid of these desirable characteristics, but they can be seen as being responsible for their more general debilitation and decline. The media not only do not offer the "ideal" art, information, or education, but they are also believed to corrupt the nature of these worthy forms whenever they disseminate likenesses of them. Finally, the media must therefore corrupt us, by exposing us to ersatz or trivialized versions of art, information, and education.

By the time the reader arrives at these disturbing claims, he or she may have ceased to consider the usefulness of comparing the mass media to an idealized version of a social "good." It can appear that criticizing the mass media as inadequate art, or information, or education, gets at the core of the influence of media on individuals and on society.

As members of current American society, we share in a climate of opinion, a set of assumptions about the "good" and the "worthy" and the "valuable" in contemporary life. We also inherit the criticism of modernity discussed in Chapter 2. In this American terrain of prejudices, preferences, and concerns, the metaphors of art, information, and education serve to reference historically distinct traditions of American criticism.

By invoking a particular image of the media, a critic, consciously or unconsciously, invokes a longer, historical trajectory of commentary. This trajectory includes not only earlier media forms, but also earlier patterns of social and cultural life. When we organize media criticism around these images of art, information, and education, we find a broad, historically grounded terrain of American thought that is mobilized, if not directly acknowledged, whenever media influence is ascribed.

To imagine the media as, for example, contemporary art forms is to invoke substantially different issues than if the media are imagined as information sources, or as educational tools. Concern over what constitutes appropriate American art, or information, or education, has long bedeviled American social thought. By examining how media criticism mobilizes these longer traditions, we can explore, and question, its fundamental characteristics.

The Media as Art

"Art," like "information" and "education," is a socially constructed category, a conceptualization with its own history of assumptions. To understand how the media are envisioned and critiqued, using this image, we can explore how something called "art" has been defined in relation to particular assumptions about its creation, distribution, and consumption. We can also examine how art has been studied in the academy, and how it has been conceived of in social and cultural criticism. Finally, we can recognize the uneasy formulation of American art, with and against a European tradition.

Media criticism that proceeds from this image is, at least on the surface, an aesthetically oriented critique. It examines media fare in relation to previously established aesthetic categories, developed through the study of canonized forms of literature, drama, painting, sculpture, and music.

This critical heritage centers on textual characteristics, but tends also to encompass assumptions about art as a social practice and a social force. It mobilizes concerns that have vexed American social and cultural critics since at least the mid-nineteenth century. These concerns include issues of definition: What makes a particular form of cultural expression "art"? Further, how can we distinguish good art and bad art? This critical heritage also includes consideration of the relationships between art and society: Does "great art" require an aristocratic tradition? If so, can there be egalitarian art? Much of the debate about American art involves an attempt to define and promote a uniquely American art that is also "good."

The recent ruptures in academic considerations of *all* forms of culture have made these questions particularly acute. Poststructuralist theory, sometimes also known as "critical theory," seems to put everything up for reconsideration—Are there texts? Authors? Readers? Genres? Who forms the canon, and for what purposes? Where does meaning reside? These are questions that bedevil current cultural thought, at least in the academy. The very positing of a definite, circumscribed arena called "art" can seem, these days, naive.

While these rumblings are affecting the ways in which literary, social, and mass-mediated "texts" are studied and evaluated in universities, they have not yet exorcised the issue of "art" from media criticism. The history of aesthetic evaluation is a tenacious one, and whether or not the term *art* is employed in the discussion, the question of the aesthetic value of media fare continues to haunt commentary.

In fact, much of the perceived "crisis" in humanistic scholarship can be connected with issues emerging from the scholarly study of media. Film and broadcasting study, conceived of as a humanistic discipline, logically connected to a liberal arts tradition, forces questioning of canonicity, of defining some forms of culture as "worthy" and others as "unworthy."

These difficult issues are foregrounded in media study, especially in attempts to justify a curriculum to skeptical colleagues in more established disciplines, heirs to canons and traditions and judgments of worth. It is difficult to convince a Milton scholar that television content should be called, or analyzed like, "art." It is also difficult to figure out the criteria by which some forms of media (foreign films, literary magazines) are more like art, and others (slasher movies, *People* magazine) not.

Some media forms that were once "not art," like Chaplin comedies, have since become "art" in academic circles—could "artness" be, then, an ascribed quality, not dependent on inherent qualities? The slippage in the certainty of aesthetic criteria, raised in the study of media content, seems to imply that anything can and should be called art, or that nothing can safely and securely be called art. This is disconcerting stuff.

In the move from novels, poems, and plays to movies, television shows, and advertising, established traditions of "artistic merit" have to be reconceptualized; this process is ongoing. In popular media criticism, the dominant tendency has been to deplore media fare as false or trivial "art." But in emerging American media scholarship, some critics are reformulating established aesthetic criteria to illuminate television in general, and individual programs in particular, while others are using the reformulations to question the foundations of aesthetic judgment.[1] These critics treat the media as an art form—of interest to us are the varying consequences of deploying the metaphor.

Timeless and Transcendent Truth
Within the academy, as well as without, there is resistance to studying the media as an art form—how can *anyone* take seriously *Magnum, P.I.* or *The Mary Tyler Moore Show* or horror films or comic books or romance novels? Continued efforts by scholars to demonstrate how these forms or genres demonstrate the evolution of complex popular aesthetics does not really dent the larger critique—that, compared to something called "art," most of what is on TV is puerile trash; most movies are sensationalistic and shallow; comic books are junk for illiterates; romance novels are sexist drivel.

What is being invoked, in this reflexive assessment of general artistic merit, is a deep commitment to certain versions of artistic worth. In spite of the attempts of particular media scholars to argue for the reconstruction of aesthetic criteria to illuminate popular art forms, it is almost impossible, in the present critical climate, to convince an outsider that media fare, in general, deserves close, careful textual analysis, that it can be treated as rich, interesting, creative, and meaningful content. Certain exceptional examples may be found (and labeled "quality television"), but the general quality of media content is deplored.

To justify such deprecation of media content, an array of notions about artistic merit is implicitly or explicitly mobilized. An excellent example of the nature and tenacity of these aesthetic criteria can be found in the 1988 report of the National Endowment for the Humanities, *Humanities in America* (Cheney, 1988).[2] The NEH report, evaluating the state of humanities education, demonstrates how aesthetic categories can function in social and cultural criticism, and how media study can be absorbed into the academy only if certain traditional criteria are acknowledged and met.

The report is the result of collaborative work—three advisory groups, fourteen regional forums, the committee chairman of the National Council of the Humanities, and other "knowledgeable people" participated in it—thus as a document it can be said to incorporate assumptions and values of mainstream commentators on the state of the humanities in American culture.

The basic tone of the report is positive, arguing that "increasing numbers of Americans are learning, are gaining the insights that the humanities offer" (Cheney, 1988, p. 4). Using the Roman definition of the humanities as "the good arts," the report considers as "good arts" those cultural forms that "serve ends beyond knowledge" (p. 4) by enlarging our understanding of the basic "moral dilemmas" and "social questions" of human existence.

The positive tone of the report is due to its assessment of an increase in the availability of, and participation in, "good" culture. The difficulties of distinguishing worthy and unworthy culture are not, apparently, troublesome—the report notes that "badly written books, terrible television programs, mindless entertainment" are indeed popular with audiences, but nonetheless, television also offers "dramatic productions and documentaries," "opera and ballet," "history, literature and philosophy from television programs that world-famed scholars have helped shape" (p. 5). In other words, television sometimes offers "good arts," unproblematically defined as the traditional "high culture" of the educated elite.

In fact, the tendency of current Marxist and/or poststructuralist criticism to question this unproblematic categorization is reprimanded. In such "political" scholarship, the report claims,

> truth and beauty and excellence are regarded as irrelevant; questions of intellectual and aesthetic quality, dismissed. "Students are not taught that there is such a thing as literary excellence as they were twenty years ago," said one faculty member recently, "we are throwing out the notion of good and bad, or ignoring it." (p. 21)

While the report acknowledges that questions about gender, race, and class are "legitimate" questions, it argues that "focusing on political issues to the exclusion of all others does not bring students to an understanding of how Milton or Shakespeare speaks to the deepest concerns we all have as human beings" (p. 21).

Thus the report assumes that certain authors (Milton, Shakespeare) automatically and unproblematically embody "truth, beauty, and excellence" and speak to universal (thus transracial, transgender, transclass, transhistorical) concerns:

> The humanities are about more than politics, about more than social power. What gives them their abiding worth are truths that pass beyond time and circumstance; truths that, transcending accidents of class, race and gender, speak to us all. (p. 27)

The NEH report considers television as a form of debased literature. The "seductive" power of television, so much "easier" than the "demanding" work of reading, are referenced via Postman (p. 29). The fate of reading, which is claimed to encourage "complex, probing, reflective ways of thinking" is at stake, due to our "national obsession" with television. Nonetheless, the report finds positive elements—television brings great literary works to the poor and uneducated, via adaptations that can be "instructive, informative, enriching." Cable television and VCRs are cited as potentially enhancing choice and control of media fare (p. 32). And finally, book sales are increasing, often stimulated by the airing of "great works" on PBS.

Aspects of Tocqueville's commentary on democratic literature, first published in 1835, are used to bring the report to a close. Here a long-standing tension is foregrounded—the tension between a democratic and aristocratic social context for art. Tocqueville (1835/1956) believed that democratic literature would be rude and untutored but nonetheless vigorous, and that it would be facile and vivid, rather than rigorous and subtle. According to the report's account, Tocqueville advocated a counterbalancing of these rude, untutored, facile, vivid tendencies of democratic art with classical literature—this Tocquevillian impulse is what the NEH report exemplifies, and applauds.

Thus, in the currents of American thought represented in the NEH report, Matthew Arnold's definition of art as "the best that has been thought or known" is mobilized. "The best" resides in particular works, usually literary, that have established membership in a canon. "The best" is timeless and transcendent; it is embodied in particular works, and calls forth in its readers or audience an ability to transcend time, space, and the "accidents" of race, gender, and class.

The American context, democratic and commercial, dominated by ("obsessed with") television, is defined as a risky but invigorating one. Yes, there is a demand for "mindless entertainments of every sort," but there is also a demand for Melville, Whitman, Twain. These are deemed worthy authors by virtue of the "comprehensive vision" they offer of the essential aspects of human nature and thought. These examples of "American classics" are "the great ideas and texts of the past [that] can enrich every life." In a democracy, the "good arts" can renew feelings and ideas, enlarge sympathies, and allow the life of the mind to thrive.

This view, then, is of art as a separate, transcendent, ennobling, and enriching sphere—somehow separate and distinct from "life." Art inspires and uplifts, because it embodies the timeless, transcendent truths glimpsed by great artists and made available to us through their works.

This view of "art" as separate from "life" is fairly common—it is a distinction between everyday, commonplace experience, seen as partial, distracted, petty, and grubby, and artistic expression, seen as complete, intense, grand, and pure. Art can enhance and deepen life because it expresses, and thus makes accessible, the deeper, truer "meanings of life." Thus art becomes inherently redemptive, a way to transcend the grubby everyday realities of material existence. Art, as the NEH report implies, is seen as a way to commune with the timeless truths of human experience.

This is the view that the poet Randall Jarrell (1961) takes in his essay "A Sad Heart at the Supermarket." In this elegaic piece, Jarrell distinguishes between Art and Life, and suggests that "the Medium" has now come between them, and between us. For Jarrell, the Medium is modern, mass-mediated culture—the specious new condition that substitutes for *both* Life and Art. As the Media become our environment, we come to define ourselves by and through the Medium, losing our ability to experience Life fully or respond to Art fully. In a memorable phrase, Jarrell suggests that we are being simultaneously starved and stuffed to death—starved for meaning (artistic and lived) and stuffed by meaning (commercial and mediated).

Jarrell's poignant argument depends on positing a separation between "art" and "life," and on a view of the Medium as coming between them, preventing their "natural" relation. The Medium is corrupt and corrupting; unlike Life, it is neither honest nor spontaneous; unlike Art, it is neither insightful nor uplifting. What we see, then, is the positing of an untainted Life that is vivified and enlarged by a sublime Art; this relation is deformed by the Medium, a commercial interloper, masquerading as a synthesis of Art and Life, but fully connected to neither.

This presumed separation of art and life also underlies émigré philosopher Hannah Arendt's (1971) critique of mass culture, in her essay "Society and Culture." Arendt makes a strong case for the differences between entertainment (which relates to people and is a "phenomenon of the life") and culture (which relates to objects and is a "phenomenon of the world"). Entertainment, for Arendt, is a necessary part of the life cycle, evaluated in terms of freshness and novelty, designed to be used up, to be consumed. Culture, on the other hand, is designed to be permanent, is evaluated in relation to its ability to grasp and move us across the ages, and cannot and should not be "consumed" as entertainment.

Arendt's concern with "the Medium" is with its ransacking of cultural objects, transforming them from permanent "things of the world" into transient "things of life"—entertainment. It is popularization and vulgarization that concerns her, because great works can, she believes, survive centuries of neglect, but they cannot survive their transformation into entertainment.

When we combine the views of the NEH report and those of Jarrell and Arendt, we see that "art" is viewed as distinct from "life": "art" is deemed transcendent, timeless, ennobling, "of the world," and art becomes that which enriches life. Under this formulation, mediated content is evaluated in terms of its ability to enrich life like art, and is found wanting.

For the NEH, the media are merely conduits, conduits that tend to show "drivel" but sometimes show "good arts" like ballet and opera. For Jarrell, the media are a polluting force that cultivate us as starved/stuffed philistines, unable to participate fully in either Life or Art. For Arendt, the media form a voracious machine that ransacks the past for cultural objects it can transform, re-present, and thus destroy forever.

As these arguments suggest, once a separate sphere of art is posited, the media can be criticized as inadequately transmitting it, or as polluting it, or as destroying it. The media become, under this metaphor, an inadequate, tainted, destructive force, one that disrupts the redemptive potential that art has for life.

Cultural Levels

Positing a separate sphere for something called "art" requires the positing of other categories for other forms of culture. Since not all cultural production is deemed "art," other descriptors are needed to define other kinds of symbolic creative expression. The notion of "levels" of cultural material—from high to low—is already familiar from Macdonald. Somewhere in between "art" and "trash" is mass culture or popular culture or media culture—not always "trash," but certainly not "art."

This resistance to calling media fare "art," and the necessity for positing various gradations of culture worth, needs to be unpacked. The reasoning behind timeless aesthetic criteria is most evident in the mass culture debate, the series of essays and articles written in the 1950s and early 1960s by, mostly, the New York intelligensia. In defining and defending art *against* media fare, commentators reveal the aesthetic assumptions they are using to critique the media.

Dwight Macdonald (1962) was an integral voice in the mass culture debates. As we have seen, for him, the term *art* is still somewhat problematic—he uses instead "High Culture," and implies that it is, however, a broad category, one that contains much that is "undistinguished . . . a few plums in a pudding of mediocrity" (p. 4).

Yet, remember, Macdonald believes that High Culture is distinguishable from Masscult and Midcult by particular criteria—Masscult is commercial and formulaic, "ground out" for a mass audience, while Midcult masquerades as High Culture, but is in fact recognizable (by Macdonald at least) as a cheap imitation. Folk Art, which Masscult and Midcult displace, is a worthy art form with much in common with High Culture.

The main thrusts of the mass culture debate were to characterize the differences between "art" and mass-mediated culture and to consider the implications of the predominance of "mass culture" for modern society. Sociologist Edward Shils (1971) posits three levels of culture, evident since time immemorial:

superior, mediocre, and brutal. His argument is that there has always been what he calls "cultural dissensus," levels of culture characterized by differing amounts of subtlety, truth, beauty, and complexity in their content.

Crucially, Shils maintains that these different levels appeal to different levels of people, who vary in their cognitive and appreciative capacities. He suggests that superior culture is not in great danger from "mass culture," and that it is up to intellectuals (like Macdonald's "we happy few") to maintain the vigor and energy of intellectually worthy forms.

Shils's levels are roughly equivalent to everyday understandings of what constitutes high, medium, and low cultural forms. But are such distinctions so easily made? On what are they based? Shils claims a kind of natural variation, corresponding to natural variations in human appreciative capacities. Is this true of symbolic material and of us?

According to Shils, each cultural level varies in the amount of subtlety, truth, and beauty it can convey. But a more careful reading suggests connections between the ascribed cultural level and the social status of producers and consumers, as well as the tendency to value old, European, metropolitan, and institutionally approved forms over current, widely popular, rural, or indigenous American forms. Clearly, more is going on in the ascription of cultural "worth" than clear cut, inherent aesthetic characteristics.

When the media are criticized as being Midcult or mass culture, a complex heritage of social, political, and economic arguments is obscured, but not banished. There is inescapable elitism in ascribing cultural worth only to those forms that are produced and enjoyed by the rich, the educated, the European, and the powerful, and in denigrating those forms produced and enjoyed by the middle and working class, the poor, the American. Describing contemporary culture as having hierarchical worth, and assuming that the media purvey the middle and lower levels, automatically sets up a denigration of media content as less worthy and less valuable.

Herbert Gans, in his book *Popular Culture and High Culture* (1974), attempts to avoid the elitist implications of cultural levels. After summarizing the available critiques of mass culture, he argues for considering cultural levels in relation to coherent taste cultures and taste publics—high culture, upper-middle culture, lower-middle culture, low culture, and quasi-folk low culture. He wants to view these as neutral descriptors, focusing on the different characteristics of each, without aesthetic evaluation.

Ultimately, Gans argues for "aesthetic relationism," where each taste culture is evaluated in relation to its ability to meet the aesthetic needs of its public, and deemed equally worthy. However, Gans also feels that American society should "maximize educational and other opportunities for all so as to permit everyone to choose from higher taste cultures" (p. 128). He wants policies that encourage the possibilities of cultural mobility, inevitably "upward." Gans thus sees education as redemptive, in that it will ensure better cultural choices by the populace.

In relation to media criticism, then, the media can be criticized as failing to include enough high culture (the NEH critique) but also as failing to represent fully the varieties of "taste publics" in the audience. The first critique is the conservative critique, the second is the liberal critique—the media neither offer enough of the best from the past nor meet the various extant or potential aesthetic desires of the people.

Aesthetic Communities

Connected to Gans's notion of taste publics is a vision of aesthetic community, groups of people bound by shared tastes and values. This vision of community underlies much of the criticism of the media as debased art—it appears most frequently when critics are attempting to prove that media fare is corrupt and commercial.

As discussed above, Macdonald believes that both High Culture and Folk Art share a set of relations between producer and audience. Artistic expression is an individual creation of an aesthetic product that makes demands of the audience and offers them some kind of "aesthetic experience." The creator and audience share a communal set of standards, standards imitated but not honored by Midcult, and unknown and uncared for by the Masscult producer.

This focus on the producer-audience relationship, with an implicit connection to the "demands" of the content for the audience, is another feature of American media criticism from the perspective of art. The popular audience is often deemed unable to appreciate the "artist" fully—if a work is accessible and popular it is less highly valued, since, if everyone "gets" it, it must be simplistic, simpleminded, appealing to the "lowest common denominator."

Again, a complicated social critique underlies an apparently aesthetic discussion: Does limited popularity assure worth? Why? What are the benefits of small, intimate connections between artist and audience? Why is a large, distanced audience mistrusted? What is so damning about popularity?

The historian Oscar Handlin makes the clearest case for the consequences of differences in communal relations between artist and audience. Handlin values the communal relationship, the celebration of shared values that exists both between the artist and his or her coterie and between the folk performer and his or her fans—in both cases there is face-to-face intimacy and mutuality, an egalitarian participation in creative expression. Handlin contrasts this with the distanced, impersonal address of the mass media, which, designed to appeal to the lowest common denominator, speak to everyone and thus to no one; they "address the empty outline of the residual American." This view of the media, as being calculated and impersonal, contrasts with the supposedly spontaneous and personal nature of communal artistic expression. Again, a worthy aesthetic form (natural, friendly, spontaneous, and communal) is imagined and compares unfavorably with its ascribed opposite—unworthy media content, unnatural, false, calculated, and alienating.

The Myth of the Artist

In the dichotomy between "art" and "media" the creator becomes either an artist, who freely and individually creates a work that "speaks" to a particular audience, or a hack, who cranks out formulaic pabulum designed to garner the largest possible audience. The artist's goal is supposedly to express his or her innermost convictions, thus offering content that will challenge and uplift the audience; the hack's goal is to figure out what the audience wants and give it to them, no matter what.

In this mythology, artists do not seek to please an audience, but only themselves. They are possessed of an inner creative fire that must be offered to the world. They do not seek to make a profit, but only to be able to continue to create. Artists who seek profit or fame have "sold out," have been co-opted—become as self-serving and unartistic as media drudges cranking out formulae. In this vision of culture creator, an individualistic, spiritual quest (the artist) is contrasted with a corporate, material existence (the media hack).

Obviously, the view of art deployed in media criticism is a surprisingly romantic one. Few current art historians, critics, and scholars would publicly make such earnest, idealistic claims for the nature, power, and purpose of creative endeavor. Yet, in media criticism, this romantic myth of the nature of art is consistently proffered, a view that sees artists as in tune with timeless truths, art objects as having the ability to uplift and ennoble, and art itself as a pure sphere able to enrich and redeem everyday life.

Similarly, a notion of artistic community is developed, one that romanticizes folk art in similar ways. Folk artists are in tune with "the people," the salt of the earth, their cultural performance speaks directly and spontaneously to their audience, giving them strength, courage, and solidarity.

In criticism that proceeds under this metaphor, the mass media are neither high art nor folk art, but some corrupted, commercialized version of each. They are seen, often, as antithetical in every way to high or folk art—media fare is mundane, trivial, transient; it calls up in us the lowest, basest, crudest emotions; it is calculated, planned, impersonal, mechanistic; it degrades us and distances us from each other, from life, and from art.

The positing of the media in opposition to art parallels a positing of modernity in opposition to tradition. This is most unmistakable when the media critique confronts the issue of community and idealizes a notion of communal connectedness that media fare somehow cannot offer. A natural, spontaneous, and uplifting communal force (art/tradition) is contrasted with a commercial, calculated, degrading, alienating force (media/modernity). This parallel is not happenstance—the terms in which the media are critiqued are the terms in which we critique modern life.

American Faultlines

I have argued, so far, that media criticism based in a metaphor of art mobilizes a particular array of ideas, values, and beliefs. It invokes a discernible pattern of concerns, ascribing to art an ability to embody timeless, transcendent truths, to appeal to the higher or better nature of its audience, to be created by an individual beholden only to his or her own loyalty to transcendent truths. This highly romantic view of art is invoked to explore how the media are *not* art, are instead degraded, less worthy cultural forms. Unlike true art, the media are deemed to be transient and immanent, appealing to lower faculties, created for profit in order to be popular.

When hierarchies of cultural forms are posited, the "higher" levels are deemed to be more complex, demanding, and subtle, requiring more skill, education, and cognitive capacity than the "lower" levels. The wider the popularity of a particular cultural item, the more likely it is to be deemed a "lower" form, since it is accessible to so many.

The inescapable elitism of this view disconcerts American critics. The mass culture debate, with its levels and hierarchies and definitions of worthy and unworthy cultures is obviously a transposed aristocratic system, with class transformed into taste-based status and worth ascribed most readily to European cultural forms from the past.

American critics, raised in a populist tradition that celebrates the value and virtues of the common man, must find some way to define and defend quality and worth in cultural content *and* in the audience—to justify their own dislike of media content without calling all those who like it dolts and idiots. This populist impulse is troublesome in American media criticism. Ultimately, it forces an elaborate justification of antipopular aesthetic evaluations and sets up a dramatic attack on the baleful influences of the media on popular taste.

The Problem of Democratic Art

As we have seen, the aesthetic underpinnings of American media criticism explicitly and implicitly revere tradition, seek conservation, set up a hierarchy of taste, and imply a mistrust of, if not a dislike for, popular choices. These are troublesome tendencies in American thought, where tradition, conservation, hierarchy, and elitism are vestiges of a repudiated European heritage.

Because of its origins, the United States has precious little indigenous cultural history. The United States was founded on a revolutionary mistrust of an aristocratic tradition and claims for itself a faith in the natural worthiness of the "common man."

American approaches to art, and to culture in general, are defined by a chronic unresolved tension between the "natural" and the "cultivated." This tension can be translated into a tension between liberal ideals and aristocratic yearnings, between a vernacular or an imported culture, between practical and aesthetic purposes. Critics and commentators choose different terms, but locate a similar dichotomy between an untutored (but passionate and spontaneous) American "natural spirit" and an educated, elaborated (but genteel and affected) European "cultivation." Thus Carl Bode (1965), in his role as interpreter of American popular literature to London literary society, can end an essay on "The American Imagination" with this paragraph:

> And that imagination has its deficiencies, without doubt. It is sometimes grotesque, often naive. But it is never pale, never passive. It has the vigor, the variety, and the creativity to justify anyone's attention. (p. 255)

This current duality in evaluating American culture—it is deficient and naive, but also vigorous, various, and creative (never pale or passive)—can be traced well back into the nineteenth century. Locating a "true" American culture, defining its value and its worth in relation to Western European traditions, tracing the differences between "imported" and "vernacular" art, critiquing the supposedly false gentility of Europhiles, understanding how commerce and industry connect to creativity and artistry, describing the differences between "true" and "fashionable" taste, defending American art forms as worthy in spite of their comparative "crudeness"—these are some of the themes of American cultural theory as it develops in the nineteenth century.

This cultural theory forms an unacknowledged backdrop to twentieth-century criticism of the mass media. Romantic assumptions about redemptive potentials of art are mobilized in some forms of media criticism—these assumptions are related to a longer, and deeper, history of American ambivalence about the location of virtue. Does virtue reside in nature? Can it also reside in culture? This backdrop also includes a long, deep history of self-justification of American "vigor" in relation to European "decadence."

The intellectual currents that fed into the founding of the United States were Enlightenment beliefs about the inherent redemptive potential of Nature. As Leo Marx (1976) persuasively argues, America was founded in assumptions that the land, seemingly timeless, infinite, and abundant, gave inherent virtue to its new inhabitants. The Enlightenment faith in natural man, freed from the artificial confines of stratified society and superfluous institutions, combined with a belief that God's laws were revealed via Nature, making "natural" a spiritualized state of virtue. If Nature is virtue, then "cultivated" becomes an ambiguous category.

To be "cultivated," educated in Europe, saturated with high culture, is to risk being seen as effete and affected. And yet, being uneducated and unfamiliar with these forms is to risk being seen as crude and crass. The way out of the dilemma was to invoke the possibility of "natural" aesthetic taste. Just as the manners of the nineteenth century were either "fine" (based in spontaneous impulses) or "fashionable" (based in established conventions),[3] so were aesthetic judgments. The American people could have basically sound, reliable, but uncultivated aesthetic taste, and this potential "democratic taste" could be celebrated in opposition to the artificial, convention-bound affectations of a European aristocratic tradition.

The development of a truly vernacular, truly "democratic" art is posited throughout the nineteenth century as a not-yet-developed possibility. By the early twentieth century, some critics are suggesting that there *is* a worthy American vernacular tradition (located in the nineteenth century) waiting to be recognized and celebrated.[4] Early twentieth-century literary and social critics are waiting either for its renewal or its full flowering, after its deflection by the material and commercial imperatives of the Industrial Revolution. Thus especially the progressive critics take up a hope for a reinvigorated culture, based in Emerson, Whitman, Thoreau, and Melville, but responding to the exigencies of twentieth-century life.

This hope for an invigorated vernacular culture, truly democratic, enlarging and animating the American people, can be seen as yet another ideal against which media content has been compared and found wanting. Not only were the media not "high culture," as discussed above, but they were also not the robust, dynamic, invigorating version of democratic culture that American critics had so long hoped for.

Take, for example, Whitman's (1871/1959) essay on the nature and possibility of democratic culture, "Democratic Vistas." It is a call for the creation of a genuine American culture, "native" and "first-class." It contrasts an ideal Literatus against the mass media of his time, which offer only

> objects, to amuse, to titillate, to pass away time, to circulate the news, and rumors of news, to rhyme, and read rhyme . . . success (so-called) is for him or her who strikes the mean flat average, the sensational appetite for stimulus, incident persiflage, etc., and depicts to the common caliber sensual, exterior life. To such, or the luckiest of them, as we see, the audiences are limitless and profitable. (pp. 487-488)

Whitman writes of the possibility of a Divine Literatus, nourished in the "rude and coarse nursing beds" of the vernacular of farmers, boatmen, miners, and mechanics throughout America. Flowers of "genuine American aroma" must spring up, offering "fruits truly and fully our own," if the crass materialism of nineteenth-century American culture is to be counterbalanced by the spiritual power of a democratic aesthetic. If this counterbalance is *not* made, "we are on the road to a destiny, a status, equivalent, in its real world, to that of the fabled damned" (p. 500).

Whitman's essay raised desires and concerns that continue to figure in cultural criticism well into the twentieth century. He makes a distinction between material and spiritual worlds that again gives art the power to redeem life. He also criticized the developing mass-mediated American culture, designed to "amuse, titillate, to pass away time," written for the "mean flat average, the sensational appetite"—the kind of literature that makes lots of money.

Whitman criticizes, too, the "fashionable" literature of the period, "highly refined imported and gilt-edged themes, and sentimental and butterfly flights, pleasant to orthodox publishers" (pp. 491-492). His ideal democratic literature is neither crude and sensationalist nor genteel and effete—neither of the supposed worst characteristics of the vernacular and the imported culture. It is, instead, an American form of an ideal folk culture. Whitman's Divine Literatus is a dream of a robust, passionate, redemptive American poetic genius, waiting to be fully realized.

The Problem of Democratic Taste

Whitman, poet of the common man, champions the untapped potential of Americans to respond to a truly Devine Literatus, once it is fully developed. Whitman acknowledges the "crudeness, vice, and caprices" of the reading public, but seems to believe these will be sloughed off when counterinfused with the spiritual power of authentic American aesthetics.

So one way to avoid a criticism of popular aesthetic choices is to suggest, as Whitman does, that the American people have simply not yet had the chance to partake of the ideal, robust, genuinely American culture he envisions (and represents). This suggestion that there is an untapped potential, in the audience, to appreciate genuine and virtuous American cultural forms is more easily made in Whitman's time than in our own.

By the early twentieth century, Whitman's second theme— the overwhelming of spiritual impulses by materialistic forces— is more fully developed. The people are still not seen as *innately* crude or capricious, but, instead, their "natural good taste" has been deflected by the mechanistic regime of industrial development, and by the commercial media that have accompanied it. Thus Frank can argue, in *The Rediscovery of America* (1929), that popular taste has been deflected by the "mechanical inner Jungle" of our lives, and by the "comfort-devices hawked by the slaves of Power"—that is, the mass media. He describes mediated culture as

> the intelligence formed in the rhythm of the movie, radio, motor, journal; fed by the mush and poison of purveyors whose aim is the nerve-drugging, mind-drugging stuffs that will make the public cry for more. (pp. 227-228)

The public (who should be the discriminating seekers of Whitman's Divine Literatus) is instead drugged and poisoned into crying for more, thanks to the "rhythm" of the media.

What develops, then, in the twentieth century, is a view of "the people" as *having been forced to become* insensitive to art, therefore unable to display the robust and natural "good taste" ascribed to them. "The people" are portrayed as helpless victims—their "crudeness, vice, and caprice" having been pandered to so often that they have become desirous of crass and sensationalistic cultural material.

Some confluence of geography, history, and biography, apparently, makes the American people "naturally" responsive to a posited new form, "democratic art." In the nineteenth century "the people" could be seen as being *as yet* relatively untutored and uncultivated, but nonetheless robust, energetic, practical, and passionate. They could be defined as a popular audience who would respond to worthy, yet-to-be-developed forms of American art.

By the twentieth century, when audiences have been vigorously responding to newspapers, magazines, vaudeville, and circuses, and as they were eagerly embracing film and broadcasting, the defense of their "natural" good taste became more strenuous. *Worthy aesthetic responsiveness was no longer an "untapped potential" but rather a deflected, even a deformed, capability.*

As we shall see in the section below on the media as education, the mass media become seen as the cause of this "deformation" of democratic taste. The media, not "the people," are blamed for the flourishing of cultural forms that are deemed, by the critics, to be neither high culture nor truly democratic culture. The undeniable fact of the popularity of certain "unworthy" cultural forms has to be explained, in American cultural thought, as due not to the unworthiness of the people, but instead to the invasive influence of outside forces.

Summary

It has been shown that American media criticism, under the metaphor of art, is characterized by an essentialist view, in that it implies that "art" is something that inheres in particular objects and that has the power to transform and redeem everyday life. These powers and possibilities can be diluted or deflected if the objects are popularized or prepared for mass consumption.

We have seen, too, how under this metaphor, individual creativity and aesthetic community are idealized. Both folk art and high art are seen as having authentic, communal connections between creator and audience, and thus having value. Mass art is deplored as being impersonal and crass, pandering to the "lowest common denominator" rather than expressing the spontaneous, creative impulses of the individual creator.

We have also seen how the ideal of a truly democratic American art has informed American cultural criticism. Democratic art is an ideal, imaginary cultural form, one that is neither commercial nor effete, neither mass art nor high culture. The media can be critiqued as being neither traditional high culture nor this imagined possibility. Media criticism proceeds in relation to a heritage of perceived American cultural promise.

Finally, we have seen how the nature of American cultural mythology makes the criticism of popular taste a difficult enterprise. "Imported" culture can be derided as calculated, genteel, fashionable, unworthy of, and inappropriate for, a natural, spontaneous, passionate democratic people. Yet, the seemingly crude, sensationalistic, commercially successful culture is widely popular—how can this be? The people rightly turn against the effete imported art, but then, mystifyingly, seem to choose "mind-drugging stuffs" for mere amusement.

Since "the people" (by virtue of their "Americanness") are supposed to have natural aesthetic capacities, equally distributed and available, the American critic must find some reasonable way to explain why "unworthy" cultural forms are popular. This lays the foundation for the gist of the critique of media as education—the media are blamed not only for their influence on art as content, but also for their ability to disrupt aesthetic sensitivities.

In short, under the metaphor of art, media influence becomes a multifaceted and extraordinarily useful scapegoat. The media adulterate worthy art forms, thus making them incapable of uplifting us; they disseminate less worthy cultural forms, thus drowning us in distracting trivia; finally, they seduce, then deform us, thus preventing us from being able to exercise our natural aesthetic judgment.

It seems as if the critics are saying that, were it not for the deformation of media influence, the American people would not only respond to, but might even spontaneously create, the much-heralded, long-awaited, but never quite realized "democratic art." The shape of American media criticism under this metaphor requires the positing of a displaced ideal, a form of culture that has all the valuable characteristics of essential "art" plus all of the valuable characteristics of "democracy."

The Media as Information

Imagining the media as sources of information mobilized a very different metaphorical heritage in American media criticism. The information metaphor is interested in the transmission of messages, not the creation of meanings; it is concerned with degrees of accuracy, not with levels of aesthetic merit. "Information" is a modern, even a bureaucratic, construct, intimately connected to a developing industrial image of a mass democratic society.

The information model engages a *transmission* view of communication; it is based in an implicitly linear model of messages moving across space. This model can be contrasted with what Carey (1989) has termed a *ritual* view of communication, based in the participatory creation of meanings in time. This ritual view is compatible with the "media as art" and "media as education" metaphors, since both rely (at least implicitly) on definitions of communication as socially constructed, communally shared, and interpretively apprehended meaning, expressive, symbolic, and self-cultivating.

The transmission view, in contrast, sees communication as a transportation between two points, as a process with a "sender" and a "message" and a "receiver." Mass communication, then, becomes a process with a single sender and multiple receivers. The media become channels or conduits for "messages"; the mass media distribute, from certain senders, particular messages to many receivers.

Under this linear view of the communication process, then, the media are evaluated in relation to their ability to transmit information clearly, comprehensively, and completely. This is an image of the mass media as *information conduits*. What is at stake, under this metaphor, is how faithfully the media depict the "real world." Reality portrayal, rather than aesthetic worthiness, is the key concern in this information metaphor.

Concern about the portrayal of reality, via the conduits of the mass media, centers on news. Journalism becomes the focus of the criticism under this metaphor, because journalism represents, in American media criticism, public information. The news process has come to be defined as the public information process, and expectations of what information can do and be are placed onto journalism as the essential modern American information practice.

This metaphor rests on beliefs so fundamental that the media criticism it engenders seems indisputable. Of *course* the news media need to be "fair" and "unbiased" and "accurate." In fact, the prospect that they might be, inescapably, unfair, biased, and inaccurate is frightening. But why? A particularly American heritage of beliefs is being mobilized in the expectation that the media must be "objective" or all is lost.

Notice how similar assumptions of verisimilitude are not made about "art." Few ask that contemporary painting, music, literature, theater, or sculpture be fair, unbiased, and accurate. This seems to be because we think of art as an experience, not an account—as an emotional, not a rational, encounter. When we think of the mass media as "our primary information source," we then demand that it be an appropriate "window on the world" and find fault with it when, in Postman's (1985) terms, it becomes instead a "funhouse mirror."

As with the media-as-art charge that media content should be of higher aesthetic quality, the chronic, unquestioned demand for "better coverage" is connected to a deep and complicated American heritage of expectations. In this case, the expectations are about journalism, democracy, and rationalism.

In order to understand the bases of the media as information metaphor, we need to examine briefly how journalism has figured in American social thought, and consider how expectations of objectivity and factuality have developed. We also need to explore the issues of representation, particularly "stereotyping," a twentieth-century criticism of entertainment programming that offers us even more insight into the expectations placed on current forms of mass communication.

In relation to news, arguments have been made about a continuing conservative bias by liberals, and a continuing liberal bias by conservatives. In entertainment programming arguments have been made for consistent biases against minorities or radical movements, for the status quo and the middle class, against the old or the corporate or the liberated or the ethnic. In study after study, prime-time television has been shown to be biased toward various political perspectives, to overrepresent violence and sex, to offer stereotypical, incomplete portrayals, and to underrepresent minority viewpoints.

What are we to make of these findings and the obvious criticisms that spring from them?

Theoretical Underpinnings

The media as information model has dominated American mass communication research. It offers a ready-made research agenda—comparisons between portrayal and actuality. It also offers a fairly straightforward model of the communication process (linear, with distinct moments or phases) and a straightforward experimental approach to influence: What are the "impacts" of particular messages, under particular conditions, from particular senders, for particular receivers?

But the media as information model offers more than just a research agenda for American communication scholars. It is also the dominant critical perspective among popular as well as scholarly critics. It is the metaphor that underlies Boorstin's argument directly, and Ewen's argument indirectly. As a metaphor, it is extraordinarily compelling.

Boorstin (1972) charges the media with being utterly inadequate information conduits. In his view, the media offer comforting illusion in the guise of information. Claiming to report reality, they give, instead, pseudo-events. This argument is paralleled somewhat by Ewen, for a different purpose. In Ewen's (1976) account, the media offer comforting illusions in the guise of information about products in the world (advertising), information that is in fact propaganda for capitalism. The illusion masks the reality of capitalist oppression. For both Boorstin and Ewen, then, a key concern is that illusory images are masquerading as neutral, trustworthy information—we are being "misled" by messages from senders who do not have our best interests at heart.

In the earlier discussion of Boorstin's and Ewen's argument, many of the key characteristics of the media as information metaphor were mentioned. First, it relies on a linear transmission model of communication. Crucially, this reliance assumes that there is a "real world" out there, concrete and comprehensible, waiting to be reported on fully. It assumes that a complete and accurate account is possible, and that such accounts are in themselves necessary and valuable. Under this metaphor, the media are expected to be perfect mirrors of, or windows on, reality. They are expected to offer us representative, accurate messages about the "world out there."

These expectations are based on an assumption so "natural" as to be almost invisible in the critique—of *course* there is a "real world" out there that can be neutrally and completely pictured, described, and thus transmitted to others. This assumption is a visual one, of a picturable reality, "out there" distinct from us, to be directly and unproblematically apprehended.[5]

This positivist perspective can be contrasted with an interpretive approach, one that claims that the word is constantly being made and remade, because we ourselves are inevitably interpretive beings, "making sense" of a world that we apprehend symbolically.[6] This is a more oral-aural model, one that invokes speech, not vision, one that sees conversation, not depiction, as the communicative impulse. In an interpretive perspective, we impose coherence on the world, we make it into stories, we are human by virtue of a narrative impulse that inescapably creates and apprehends symbolic representations that cannot, and need not, directly mirror or mimic a neutral, solid, separate "real world."

The information metaphor, based on a transmission model, makes very different assumptions about the world and about the role of communication within it. In the information model, we, as individuals, become rational knowledge seekers and evaluators, not interpretive symbolizers; media content is made up of discrete, analyzable message components, not "stories" and "discursive formations"; senders seek to "inform" or "persuade" receivers, not to regale or rejuvenate (and certainly not to "sustain reality" with) audiences. The world exists, and communication is a necessary process within it. In contrast, under a ritual view, "the world" is known only in and through communication; it is "the means by which reality is produced, maintained, repaired and transformed" (Carey, 1989, p. 23).

These two views are fundamentally different and fundamentally incompatible. They have sometimes been faultily characterized, in discussions of media theory and scholarship, as the distinction between quantitative and qualitative research, or between social science and the humanities approaches, or between administrative and critical researchers. Such distinctions are misleading, but the impulse is understandable—to locate and describe apparent differences in research questions, research methods, and research conclusions. These differences are best understood, I believe, as based in a deep epistemological division. Once these epistemological distinctions are understood and acknowledged, findings within the different traditions can be located and understood in their appropriate contexts.

The transmission model, linked (loosely) with quantitative, social science, and/or administrative research traditions, informs the bulk of the academic research on representation, and some of the research on news biases. But the information metaphor has intellectual connections to nineteenth-century social and political thought, when information became popularized and transformed under industrialization, and was mobilized as justification for a particular kind of journalism, and for a particular kind of modern democracy.

News as Modern Information

What is particularly intriguing about the media as information model is that it engages historically locatable assumptions about the nature and necessity of "news" in contemporary life. This means that we can trace how objectivity became a news value, and then suggest how "factuality" becomes a criterion for general media worth.

Schudson's (1978) account of the rise of objectivity as a news value insightfully traces the connections among industrialization, technological developments, status concerns, occupational ideals, and adversarial criticism in the shaping of news values and practices. Schudson begins by noting that objectivity is a "peculiar demand" to make of a business practice (news is a profit-making enterprise) with connections to politics, and without explicit apparatuses designed to "guarantee" objectivity (as exist in law or medicine or scientific research) (p. 3). Why do we expect news to be objective?

Traditional histories of journalism trace a triumphant evolution from polemical party papers (in the early nineteenth century) to the exemplary factual journalism of the *New York Times* (in the late nineteenth century), challenged by seamy "yellow journalism" but later buttressed by the muckraking tradition (of the early twentieth century), resulting finally in a model of balanced, neutral, objective, socially responsible journalism. This "best" journalism is seen as being ever threatened by the popularity of less worthy forms of journalism, as exemplified by the tabloids, the flashy *USA Today* ("McPaper") and "happy talk" television news. In short, traditional histories tell of the development of an ideal model of news as objective information, against perceived continuous threats from cheap, trashy, entertainment-oriented alternatives.

In Schudson's retelling of the historical development of news practices, the focus is on news as a historically locatable product, shaped and defined in changing social, cultural, and institutional conditions. Journalism becomes a profession as news becomes a commercially successful business, addressing an emerging middle class via the penny papers in the mid-nineteenth century. The penny press, with its breathless accounts of crime and disaster, competed successfully against the politically affiliated six-penny papers. The model of journalism as story telling, as compelling narrative accounts constructed by the reporter for the delight of the reader, did not give way to a more neutral, information-based model until the late nineteenth century.

Schudson distinguishes between "story" and "information" models of journalism, suggesting that they vied for professional and popular legitimacy in the late nineteenth century. The distinction between the colorful, dramatic "story" journalism and the neutral, dispassionate "information" model was made, he argues, into a *moral* distinction. This distinction was a moral tension between self-indulgence and self-denial, based in class and status distinctions. These distinctions and tensions were ultimately between the middle and working classes (who favored a story model) and an educated, upwardly mobile, upper-middle class (who favored an information model).

The story model becomes labeled as "lower" and the information model as "higher" in relation to the status of the readers who prefer them and the assumed moral differences between them. Once again, as in the mass culture debate, distinctions between "emotion" and "reason" appear, with superiority automatically granted to that form of journalism that apparently appeals to reason because it does *not* appeal to emotion. "Information," a dispassionate form of communication, is seen as offering bits of knowledge to an educated readership who seek to add to their fund of knowledge in order to make better-informed decisions about the world.

Of particular interest in this context is Schudson's recognition that "objectivity" is most tenaciously celebrated *just as there is an increasing mistrust of its very possibility*. In the early twentieth century, the reliability of "facts" is being challenged by public relations, advertising, and wartime propaganda. At the same time, the reliability of "reason" is being challenged, by psychologists discovering the unconscious, and by sociologists studying crowd behavior. As the horrors of World War I radically undermine faith in rational progress and the Depression undermines faith in industrial capitalism, objectivity is seized on, by journalists and journalism critics and scholars, as the central, desirable, even mandatory feature of news.

A belief in the necessity of objective accounts becomes a way to escape the "doubt and drift" of the twentieth century,

Schudson concludes, a way to "cover over . . . the disappointment in the modern gaze" (p. 159). Objectivity becomes a kind
of talisman against uncertainty and against the self-interested
blandishments of advertising and propaganda.

This analysis clarifies the source of the widespread fears
of "subjectivity" in news accounts. "Subjectivity" is seen as
characteristic of mistrusted stories—ads and propaganda—designed to seduce and mislead. "Objectivity" is characteristic of
educated, even scientific accounts, designed to decipher disin-
terestedly the world as it is. Objective accounts can be trusted
because they are in no one's interest, they are simply "reports"
of a world that then let the public "make up its own mind"
about what those reports "mean."

Information thus becomes a kind of neutral public fund,
disseminated by professional reporters. The goal of news
should be maximum coverage of events "out there" so that
we, the public, can become "well informed enough to make a
decision." As "the world" begins to appear more and more
irrational, less and less responsive to our "decisions," less and
less peaceful, progressive, or sane, we cling ever more tightly
to a belief in the possibilities of neutral information to free us
from subjective entanglements, from the thrall of illusion and
the seeming caprice of fate.

In contrast to traditional news histories, Schudson's account
offers us a way to see news as a historically located social and
cultural practice, the "objectivity" of which is a relatively recent
development. Faith in objective information is grounded in
twentieth-century doubts about the very possibility of a rational, ordered world. Schudson implies that our desire for objective news accounts is based in an unacknowledged mistrust of
the possibility of truly objective accounts—we are repressing
doubt, engaging in a collective, quixotic "quest for certainty."

This view can be combined with analyses of the two "theories of the press" that have dominated American evaluations of
the news media. By doing so, we can suggest that news, imagined as neutral information, becomes, in twentieth-century

American social thought, a resource to preserve and bolster democracy. If we indeed cling most tenaciously to those values we unconsciously fear are being eclipsed, then Boorstin and Ewen's concern over the "objectivity" of media accounts may reference their deeper fears about the loss of democratic possibility.

Theories of an American Press

Remember that the founding conditions of the American press system were, essentially, theoretical. "Freedom of the press" was a crucial component of the libertarian theory that informed our constitutional origins. The notion of a press system free from external constraints is central to liberalism's belief in the emergence of truth and reason in free and open discussion.

What is often forgotten, however, when "freedom of the press" is invoked, is that the "freedom" being referred to is a freedom to express *opinion*—passionate, partisan statements of conviction and belief. The "open marketplace of ideas" is a marketplace of freely expressed opinion, out of which "truth" can emerge, among rational discussants. The greatest danger to this process is censorship of any kind: Curtailing the free and open circulation of opinion risks undermining the basic process of rational progress—the continuing discovery of truth via discussion of conflicting opinions.

This libertarian theory of the press was congruent with newspaper practice in the post-Revolutionary period. Politically partisan papers chronicled and circulated disparate opinions. Written in dramatic language, laden with invective, to contemporary eyes they seem extremely "biased." Colonial newspapers were expected to be carriers of opinion, to be read and discussed and responded to in kind. What needs to be understood is how this notion of the press as opinion purveyor become transformed, by the twentieth century, into a view of the press as information conduit.

The transformation has been gradual and incomplete. As we can see, much of the language of libertarian theory is still in use, even though the substance of the newspaper has changed from opinion to something called "information," a particularly modern commodity. There are never simple or systematic explanations to historical transformations, but some key influences can be located.

First, the social role of the newspaper changed, as Schudson's analysis, among others, makes clear. By the 1830s, the urban newspaper was moving from political sponsorship and circulation among the relatively well-to-do to commercial sponsorship and circulation among an emerging middle class. The contents shifted in relation to this new role. "Beats" developed, with reporters trained to cover them, to keep readers apprised of crime, city politics, scandal, high society—areas of urban life that interested readers.

The newspaper, by the mid to late 1800s, became more of a "mediator" between reader and events; the reporter functioned as the "eyes and ears" of readers who could not be everywhere for the "day's events." The written reports were colorful, dramatic, narratively compelling. They were "eyewitness" accounts, designed to make the reader feel as if he or she were "right there."

By the late nineteenth and early twentieth centuries, newspapers were coming under increasing attack for their perceived failure to act "in the public good." New expectations had developed for the American press. In the tension described by Schudson between the *New York Times* model of self-restraint (information) and the *New York Post* model of self-indulgence (entertainment) we see concerns that became fully developed in the twentieth century—concerns about the appropriate, even the necessary, role of the press in modern, industrial America.

As Peterson (1956) delineates the main charges against twentieth century news practice, they engage criticisms of the pattern of increasing scale, power, and concentrated ownership of major newspapers. According to its critics, the press uses its power for its own ends; is subservient to big business, letting advertisers control contents; resists social change; is sensational and superficial; endangers public morals; invades individual privacy; and allows access only to the business class.

As these criticisms were being made, journalism was becoming increasingly professionalized. Journalism education, professional organizations, and interest groups were developing; the practice of news was becoming both self-aware and self-defensive. This was part of a more general professionalization and an increasing emphasis on the role of experts and expertise in guiding an industrial, heading toward corporate, democracy.[7]

In response to the criticism of the press, and in congruence with an emerging image (modern professional), newspeople defined a new role for themselves. Their role was now as vital middlemen, mediating between those in power and everyday citizens. They allowed themselves to be defined (most notably by the Commission on Freedom of the Press) as having an obligation, a crucial responsibility in modern mass society. The new role of the press was to act in the perceived interest of the public, to ensure that the public had the kind of knowledge needed to make wise decisions.

Various codes of ethics were drawn up, numerous editorials were written, and gradually a new working theory of the role of the press in America emerged. The "social responsibility model" focused on the vital role of news in making modern democracy possible, and it defined information as the crucial commodity that would allow democracy to be maintained.

A cynical reading of this period would suggest that, as journalism was being assailed for its subservience to business interests, its sensationalism, and its triviality, professional journalists, in response to the critics, found a way to make their work seem both worthy and vital. By emphasizing the public's need for trustworthy and impartial information in complex modern life and demonstrating how the press was uniquely able to meet this need, they enhanced their own public credibility while getting the critics off their back.

This is, I believe, too cynical a reading. As I argue throughout this book, the media in general, and the press in particular, are sites in and throughout which we work out doubts, ambivalences, hopes, and fears about social developments. Journalism became a site, in the early twentieth century, for specific fears of concentrated ownership and commercial subservience; these fears were indirectly countered with praise for journalism's special ability to convey information to an uninformed public. Journalists became the professional purveyors, while journalism became the idealized means through which a modern "informed public" could make wise decisions.

Interestingly, the public is deemed to be much more vulnerable and lethargic under the social responsibility theory of the press than under the libertarian theory. Without the information that newspapers convey, it is implied, the public would be easily seduced by propaganda, lulled into complacency or whipped into a barbaric frenzy. Information becomes the commodity that allows reason to operate, that prevents emotion from getting free reign.

Thus, in justifying information as a necessary modern commodity, the public is defined as an otherwise uninterested and vulnerable crowd in whose interest journalists must act. This new modern mass public seems to *require* the activities of a special class of people to keep it informed. Journalism becomes the media form that can force the public to acknowledge the events of the day, because it can set appropriate agendas and keep an eye on politicians and businessmen.

Notice, then, how when the "media as information" model is invoked, a view of "the people" as needing outside agencies to maintain their decision-making abilities is also invoked. This is a far cry from the earlier libertarian model of news, with newspapers operating as opinion circulators, sparking discussion among members of the public, fostering free and open discussion, out of which social truth emerges. The information model is a fundamentally modern conception, one that sees the world as made up of powerful institutions and increasingly powerless individuals, where what sets you free is truth defined as knowledge, expertise, information.

Lippmann and Dewey

The contrast between libertarian and social responsibility doctrines can be partially refigured as a distinction between ritual and transmission views of communication, and thus also between auditory and visual metaphors. As Carey (1989, chap. 3) points out, John Dewey and Walter Lippmann represent these two distinct poles in their views of the role of the press in relation to the public. The debate between the two, as evidenced in Lippmann's *Public Opinion* (1922) and Dewey's *The Public and Its Problems* (1927/1947), is a debate between two views of communication and two views of the public.

During the early twentieth century, both Lippmann and Dewey offered visions of a new kind of journalism, one that could help deflect or transcend the weaknesses of the current kind. Both call for a new, more social scientific kind of journalism, but they mean by this very different things.

Lippmann operates from a premise that "as social truth is organized today, the press is not constituted to furnish . . . the amount of knowledge which the democratic theory of public opinion demands" (Rossiter & Lare, 1963, p. 400). Lippmann's remedy, in *Public Opinion*, is to suggest a center or bureau, a kind of running audit of analysis and record, that would be nonpartisan and based in the objective methods of science. This is "information" in its purest form. Experts such as statisticians, accountants, auditors, industrial counselors, engineers, scientific managers, and personnel administrators could provide the disinterested information that would make things intelligible to the lay public.

Under Lippmann's ideal, journalists would become professional information brokers who organize and disseminate social and political facts. Experts would be the source of these

facts, experts whose inquiry is guided by a disinterested seeking of truth. Such expert knowledge would support an objective, orderly, and comprehensive presentation of news, superior to the "dramatic, disorderly, episodic" news Lippmann
believes has come to dominate current journalism.

Dewey's concern, in contrast, is with identifying the conditions that can transform an atomized modern society into a
"Great Community." Dewey places his faith in communication
of what he calls "social inquiry." For him, "communication of
the results of social inquiry is the same thing as the formation
of public opinion." Thus we need to develop a genuine social
science as well as a new kind of news, so that

> an organized, articulate Public comes into being. The highest and
> most difficult kind of inquiry, and a subtle, delicate, vivid and
> responsive art of communication must take possession of the phys-
> ical machinery of transmission and circulation and breathe life
> into it. (p. 184)

Thus, for Lippmann, journalism is bettered if it becomes an
accurate neutral transmission of information about a complex
world, whereas for Dewey, journalism is bettered if it becomes
a "subtle, delicate, vivid and responsive art" that brings into
being a communal public. While both deplore the journalism of
their day as being inadequate, sensationalistic, and fragmented,
they offer very different solutions. Lippmann's solution involves the information metaphor; Dewey's is more congruent
with the art metaphor, in his notions of content, and the education metaphor, in relation to influence.

I have been describing how "information" is a modern value,
one that is intimately tied to the emergence of an industrial,
bureaucratic society. Information becomes a desirable commodity in relation to a set of assumptions about how the world
works, and how individuals form a society.

I have suggested that viewing communication as information transmission is an essentially linear, particularistic, and
mechanistic perspective. It is congruent with logical positiv-

ism, with a view of reality as "out there," neutral and comprehensible, waiting to be depicted by particular methods of investigation.

As the mass media developed in the twentieth century, they have been increasingly criticized as being inadequate information conduits, as failing to convey vital information appropriately from the unseen world to the public. An ideal type of journalism—dispassionate, fair, unbiased—is juxtaposed with a demonic type—passionate, unfair, biased. By the mid-twentieth century, "the facts" are seen as speaking for themselves, if framed correctly; "the facts" are to be divorced from "opinion," which muddies and distorts the truth.

Thus the history of journalism is written as a quest to attain an information goal. An ideal form of journalism is imagined and defended against the perceived chronic threat of debased (because biased, trivial, sensationalistic, entertaining) accounts. News as information is deemed a modern necessity, a way to ensure that the public has the information it requires to self-govern.

This view can be located in a social responsibility theory of the press, in contrast to the founding conditions of libertarian theory. It has been connected here to the emergence of objectivity as a journalistic ideal, which has been linked to dismaying doubts about guaranteed social progress. As faith in the possibility of reliable truth decreases, defense of the ideal of objectivity increases. The ideal of objective journalism can be seen as a talisman against uncertainty.

Finally, I have noted how the public is defined, under an information metaphor, as mere recipients of information. This relatively passive role makes the "social responsibility" of the press all the more crucial. Journalists become the proxies of the public, ferreting out necessary information, acting in our interests, for our own good, as we go about our business, trusting that we will get what we "need to know" through the daily news.

This ideal form of journalism, with its dispassionate, reliable, neutral depiction of reality, has become an unquestioned "good." Like the metaphor of media as art, a particular cultural form is seen as redemptive. Faith in the inherent value of information runs so deep that it is almost impossible to question its usefulness in contemporary life. In fact, only a sketchy portrait is given, by critics, of what will happen when the media fail to offer trustworthy information.

In, for example, Boorstin's account, the fear is that, with distorted news, we come to live in an illusory world, one that we do not even recognize as illusion. In Ewen's account, the fear is that we have come to believe the lies we are being told, and thus cannot recognize what causes our oppression. In Postman's account, the fear is that we will come to love the entertainment we are being offered in place of information—we will seek to be amused rather than informed.

For these critics, the perceived loss of reliable, neutral information is a dangerous one. Yet the danger is tied mostly to the loss of access to the supposedly accessible and desirable "reality." For Boorstin, that reality is forgotten; for Ewen, it is misperceived; for Postman, it is dismissed as boring. All three assume that there is something "out there" to which we need access. Knowing "reality" somehow gives us something vital and valuable. Information is our means to the ideal end of reality apprehension.

Information, because it is *not* self-interested, because it fosters rational rather than emotional response, because it gives us access to a neutral, reliable "world out there," can be trusted. Thus information is a crucial commodity for critics using this metaphor, a commodity necessary for individual sanity, moral progress, and the survival of modern democracies.

Information in Entertainment

This account of journalism as "ideal information" gives us some sense of why newspapers, newsmagazines, and broadcast news programs are evaluated in relation to their ability to give a full, complete, and accurate picture of the world. News, defined as neutral, reliable information, has come to be defined as a prerequisite for a modern democratic society.

But, in media criticism, this ideal of "accurate information" can also be applied to entertainment programming. Soap operas, situation comedies, and made-for-TV movies are castigated as being "unrealistic," for showing problems as resolvable or everyone as wealthy or White or middle class. Somehow the values that have emerged in relation to scientific inquiry and news reporting are applied to all media fare, particularly television content. In the current climate of opinion, even explicitly dramatic material can be castigated for failing to be "realistic."

Thus studies have been conducted that compare the percentages of women and minority groups portrayed in prime-time television with national demographics or the number of violent crimes committed on TV with the number committed in real life, or that evaluate the portrayal of particular professional groups (businessmen, lawyers) in relation to their "real" nature. At stake is the issue of stereotyping—portraying in a simplistic and insulting manner—which is connected to issues of over- or underrepresentation and issues of inaccurate or misleading representation.

The evidence is overwhelming—prime-time network television does *not* mirror American life in relation to demographics, behavior, or professions. It distorts, selects, and simplifies. The result is that particular social groups, environmental settings, professions, and circumstances are misrepresented. Medicine, law, business, university life, bartending, waitressing, child rearing, romance, city life, country life, suburban life are not, according to the critics, accurately or adequately portrayed.

But what constitutes an accurate or adequate portrayal? These charges assume there is a "reality" out there, accessible statistically, that is being purposely skewed or misrepresented. Would a statistically constructed narrative be more "true"? Probably not, since truth is more elusive than a demographic account. Whose "reality" is being promoted and whose obscured is a more fruitful line of inquiry, since so-called reality seems multiple, shifting, and capable of being told in various ways.

It is not clear whether dramatic material has ever mirrored or can now directly mirror this complex and contradictory reality. Furthermore, *should* entertainment programming mirror reality, if it could be located and agreed upon? What is interesting about the charge of inadequate portrayal is that it should be made at all. Why would we expect an inherently dramatic symbolic form, one that emerges from a longer tradition of popular entertainment, to mirror statistically determined categories? What underlies this charge that the media are dangerous because they give us such an unrealistic picture of the world?

The mass media, particularly the now-dominant medium of television, are being charged with a social responsibility similar to that of journalism. Apparently, critics are expecting the media to function as information conduits in *all* contexts and circumstances. Since television has been defined as our "primary information source," and information has come to be defined as crucial and inherently worthy, anything on television must inform us accurately. If it does not, if it gives us dramatic enhancements or distortions, gives us formulaic or insulting portrayals, then it is deemed to be failing in its responsibility.

The underlying fear is that we will come to believe that what we see on television is an accurate reflection of the world. Whether the issue is news or entertainment, the fear is that we, the audience, will confuse reality and illusion, mistake entertainment for news, trust something inherently untrustworthy, because it is subjective and emotionally charged.

Entertainment programming under the information model, is not only inadequate, but dangerous. Remember, Postman believes that entertainment is benign and amusing as long as it stays "in its place," but that it becomes extremely dangerous when it leaks into other arenas like news. Similarly, just by leaking into prime-time viewing, entertainment programming risks being mistaken for reality, at least by "the average viewer."

Hence entertainment programming can be evaluated, under the information metaphor, as inadequate and misleading. Critics, interest groups, and concerned viewers can lobby for more accurate and fair portrayals, can demand that popular shows include or exclude, even offer "positive portrayals," in the interests of fairness and representativeness.

Notice that few respected forms of culture (novels, plays, paintings, folktales) could meet the criteria being used on prime-time television by these critics. Past forms of entertainment are loaded with violence, misogyny, racism, stereotyping, sexuality. They do not, and are not expected to, mirror reality, past or present. Why this criticism now?

It seems that, under the information metaphor, expectations are placed on the entertainment media that cannot possibly be met. Even with a complete shift to a news and documentary format, complete and accurate portrayal of a unitary reality is impossible. News and documentaries are (already) critiqued for their inadequate representations, and docudramas, because of their blend of entertainment and news, constitute one of television's most maligned and mistrusted forms.

The issue of entertainment's accuracy reveals, more clearly than does the issue of news accuracy, the bases of the critique of media as information. Information is itself so trusted, so valued, and deemed so necessary in modern life that it should be characteristic of all popular culture forms. Information is inherently worthy, and entertainment is mistrusted, at least in part, because it does *not* appropriately inform.

In the media as information perspective, the media are perceived as mass conduits for information; as such, they can and should offer access to the kinds of knowledge that will increase the social good. To the extent that they do *not* offer this kind of information, to the extent that they offer instead something called entertainment, or opinion, or bias, or distortion, they are believed not only to prevent the fostering of "the good," but to increase the chances of its permanent debilitation. The failure of the media to provide accurate information about the world is seen as causing the evils of illusion, deception, and amusement, evils that prevent the development of a truly enlightened public.

The media as information critique mobilizes a view of the individual as, ideally, an informed citizen with accurate images of the world. He or she will use these images to make good private and public decisions. The metaphor of information assumes that knowledge is a transmissible commodity, from "the world" to "the individual," and that, given "enough information," good decisions can be made.

The information metaphor believes in the possibility of, and thus the necessity of, separating facts from values. It believes that neutral facts can and will "add up" to a complete story. The information metaphor inherently mistrusts subjectivity, seeing it as corrupted by opinion, bias, and self-interest. Sensational or dramatized accounts cannot be "informative" because they are passionate and persuasive, a kind of propaganda that misleads and deceives.

Under this image, we find a belief in information as value-free "facts" emanating from the world, to be collected and transmitted across space. We also find an almost talismanic faith that wide and free distribution of information will allow full and free participation in democracy.

For modern democracy to be preserved, it seems, information must be neutral, dispassionate, and complete. If the media can be made to give us an undistorted picture of the world, we, as citizens, will be able to make wise decisions in private and in public. If, however, they continue to give us an inaccurate, because distorted, picture of the world, we will be misled and confused. Based on these inadequate portrayals of the world, we will make unwise decisions, in private and in public.

In media criticism, we find evidence for a belief that information affects our perceptions, and thus affects who we are and what we are capable of. Information is thus similar in influence to art, even though the site of its influence is different. Art, as we have seen, is deemed to influence our spiritual capacities rather than our cognitive abilities. Art, it is believed, engages an aesthetic sensibility, while information engages a rational, evaluative one.

Yet both the art and the information metaphor, ultimately, assume influence on us as individuals. The dire consequences of media influence, under both these metaphors, relies on a conceptualization of the media as forms of response—as modes of being and becoming. This conceptualization can be considered an "education" metaphor, and it is to that metaphor that we now turn.

The Media as Education

The image of the media as an educational force overlaps with images of the media as art forms and as information sources. It partially combines these images, blending images of transmission (what kinds of messages, values, meanings are being taught?) with images of cultivation (what kinds of people are being "grown" by the media?). The central issue, under this image, is *who we become* if the media are our primary educational institution in society.

"Education," as a social construct, has its own historical trajectory of values, beliefs, and assumptions, connected with but different from the trajectories of "art" and "information." Like "the media," "education" has become an implicit touchstone for unresolved conflicts in American social, cultural, and political thought.

To understand the conflicted context of American notions of education, we need to acknowledge the heritage of first a colonial, then a radical democratic, then an urban and industrial context. Education maintains and supports colonial expansion because it makes possible the inculcation of values across space and time. English educational practices, with connections to a humanities tradition of cultural preservation, were combined with a more nationalistic individualistic faith in the value of self-education.

This notion of self-education (exemplified in Benjamin Franklin's autobiography but evidenced long after in all manner of inspirational and success literature during the nineteenth century) suggests a tension between models of education as the exposure to great works (cultivation of sensibilities) and experience in practical affairs (knowledge about the world).[8] This parallels the tension we find between the metaphors of media as art and media as information.

This tension in educational expectations can also (and again) be seen in another contrast between John Dewey and Walter Lippmann, this time in their beliefs about the ideal purposes of education. For Dewey, education should reflect the life of the larger society, cultivating students as full social citizens, lively and responsive, whereas for Lippmann, education should transmit the knowledge of experts to students trained to evaluate and reason.

In popularized versions, these two views of education still clash. Schools are charged with becoming too oriented toward socialization, ignoring the basics and turning out uninformed, illiterate students who "work well with others." Instead, some critics claim, they should be taught the fundamentals—all students should have a grounding in the basic literature of the classic tradition. At the same time, other critics fear the result of a "back to basics" movement, with students becoming unreflective drones, memorizing vast quantities of dead information, unable to make sense of or to incorporate that knowledge into everyday life. The metaphors of ritual and transmission continue to be fundamentally incompatible, wherever they appear.

What does become clear in any account of education in American life is the expectation that education functions in relation to social needs. Its essential practices are supposedly more closely allied to those of the church and the family, rather than to business. Education is deemed to be in the public interest, a crucial foundation for a free nation.

The chronic ambivalence about the increasing prevalence of vocational education, the passionate discussion of whether prayer should be allowed in the schools, the violence and furor over school busing, and the chronic "crisis" in curriculum issues all bear witness to the ambiguous role of education in American life. What ought public education to be? To do? To result in? Is it supposed to give everyone access to the fruits of civilization, thus demonstrating the egalitarian possibility of American life? Or is it supposed to make us into good and productive workers, thus ensuring our dominance in a world market? Is it supposed to help build our self-esteem, thus overcoming familial dysfunction and creating well-adjusted adults? Should it teach us to question or to support authority?

Clearly, public education is charged with a conflicting set of expectations—these conflicts also appear in the criticisms of television that emerge under this metaphor. Whatever is unresolved in discussions of education in society remains unresolved in discussions of media-in-society—there are necessary parallels in the social expectations placed on these two institutions.

Commercial Education via the Media

But a crucial difference between the two is that the media are known to seek profit, and, as such, are differently figured in the critical terrain. The fact that the media are commercially based, seeking to keep our attention, not to enlighten, inform, or improve us, is of grave concern under the education image.

The assumption is that public academic institutions, beholden to scholarly values and "the public good," are incompatible with corporate values, beholden to profit and market share. Students are educated to embody the values of democratic citizenship; consumers are educated to embody the values of capitalism. As a commercial institution, the media make us into what "the system" needs—they turn us into whatever those in power want us to be.

The chronic mistrust of the commercial system, from the Right as well as from the Left is a key feature of media criticism in general, and of the education metaphor in particular. This separation of education from commercial purposes is paralleled by a general desire to keep commercial processes walled off, separated from information and from art. The sanctity of art and information and education are seen as vulnerable to corruption or pollution via commerce.

That the media educate viewers as consumers, inculcating capitalist and/or corporate values, is a charge leveled most passionately by liberal and radical critics. This is what Ewen's argument is all about—that advertising in particular "educates" us in order to blind us to the real causes of our discontent. Advertising offers us solutions that only increase our dependence on the system that causes us pain. Whatever troubles us under corporate capitalism is turned into a condition soluble only through consumption; whatever hurts us is turned into a "situation" to be resolved only under the status quo.

Ewen develops, in relation to a history of advertising, an argument that C. Wright Mills made in 1956 in *The Power Elite*. Mills argues that the media enter into our experience of ourselves—they provide us with specious identities and aspirations, offering the techniques to achieve them and escape when we cannot. The media are a malign force, they

> do not articulate for the viewer or listener the broader sources of his private tensions and anxieties, his inarticulate resentments and his half-formed hopes. They neither enable the individual to transcend his narrow milieu not clarify its private meaning. (p. 314)

Transcendence of the narrow milieu is not offered by mass education, either. Mills's argument is that, in modern society, the media, education, and voluntary associations have *all* become impersonal, centralized, mass organizations. These large-scale organizations deepen and extend undemocratic power relations, because they mimic, rather than mitigate, the increasing centralization of power in an elite.

Mills clearly believes in the possibilities of transcendence, of being able to recognize the relationship between personal circumstances and social conditions. This critical transcendence seems to be possible, as in earlier American ideals, by a wedding of classical education with practical experience. Mills himself possesses it—he wants it to be characteristic of the masses who (in modern times) instead perceive their lives as "a series of traps."

Mills, like many other American critics who use the image of media as education to make their critique, holds out the possibility of a new and different kind of education, one that will allow viewers, readers, and listeners, to escape the pernicious educational influences of mass communication. Such a liberating education involves the development of critical faculties. Of an ability to see through the seductive fabrications of the self-interested media.

This ability to pierce the seductive veils of media education is characteristic of the critic him- or herself, but it is rarely ascribed to "them," the mass audience being cultivated by media values. Critics assume that, while they in particular have found ways to stand apart from the influences of media education, most people do not realize how they are being shaped, and in whose interests.

This blindness to media blandishments is deemed to be especially true of children, who are seen as the most vulnerable and susceptible to mediated imagery. Apparently, they have not yet had the kind of "protective" education and experience or developed the appropriate critical capacities or theoretical sophistication that would enable them to elude seduction.

Vulnerable Children

The most frequently quoted television statistic must surely be the number of hours children spend viewing television. The numbers seem to "speak for themselves." When Marie Winn (1977) says that children spend more than a third of their waking hours watching television, there is no need to evaluate this statistic further—it is "obviously" a frightening fact. But why? If, for example, a child were to spend a third of his waking hours reading, would this be an alarming state of affairs? A third of her waking hours in school? In movie theaters? Playing baseball? Reading Shakespeare? Collecting butterflies? Practicing ballet? What is it about television viewing in particular that so disturbs parents, teachers, and media critics?

The idea of children sitting silently in front of a television for hours on end, passively absorbing whatever the set shows them, distills the "media as education" image to its most disturbing essence. Vulnerable children, without the "critical skills" required to respond rationally to the commercial appeals, antisocial images, and unrealistic accounts, are being, it seems, somehow hypnotized by the television, are becoming "addicted" to the "plug-in drug."

Hypnotic Media Power

Common to much popular media criticism is an extension of this metaphor to adults. Television viewing is described as passive, addictive, and isolating, taking place alone, in a darkened room. This results in a kind of television-induced trance, where the viewer can be—against his or her will—convinced or persuaded or compelled to buy products, believe falsehoods, be led.

Some critics take this assumption to the limit. In *Four Arguments for the Elimination of Television*, Jerry Mander (1978) describes the supposed neurophysiological consequences of television technology, implying that the artificial light, the "isolated" viewing conditions, and the hypnotic images combine to make us directly vulnerable to "autocratic control." Such arguments make use of anecdotal evidence as well as selected research studies (often unsubstantiated or taken out of context) to characterize television as an overwhelmingly potent evil that has infiltrated our homes, posing innocuously as a mere household appliance.

While not all media critics are as apocalyptic as Mander about the hypnotic powers of television, the notion of "hypnosis" still pervades much of the criticism of media influence. This notion assumes a dichotomy between fully awake, conscious, rational mental activity and half-awake, unconscious, irrational responses.

We are deemed at risk when viewing television or listening to rock music or reading comic books or watching movies, because we are not alert. We are not sufficiently charged and wary of these attempts to seduce and persuade us. We become passive, enervated victims, lulled into complacency and then shaped by the forces that take over when we are least aware.

This model of media influence seems most convincing with children, but it has appeared with each newly popular technology and usually only one technology at a time is deemed to be this hypnotically powerful. Thus movies are no longer widely perceived as dangerous experiences, nor are comic books, nor is jazz or rock and roll (although specific explicit examples might be). Yet each of these mediated forms has been, in the past, charged with hypnotic power. Now heavy metal music and television have become the current demonic hypnotists—the media that are deemed to have the most druglike, addictive qualities.

Theories of Media Influence
The image of the passive, vulnerable viewer has long been criticized in academic research on media influence. Some early models of how media messages work did rely on this kind of

notion—viewers were imagined as vulnerable and easily convinced by self-interested messages. Fears of, for example, the power of propaganda to persuade masses of people, were fueled by the effective wartime use of propaganda techniques, especially in Nazi Germany. European sociological thought, especially on the behavior of "the crowd" in modern society, was congruent with these fears. Notions of hysteria, crowd contagion, and mob action and rule are aspects of this view of the media as extraordinarily powerful stimuli, and of "the people's" vulnerability to prepackaged, self-serving messages.

The so-called hypodermic needle model of media effects, which conceives of messages as being "injected" into the passive viewer, describes this view of direct, unmitigated media influence as it was retrospectively ascribed to American communication scholarship in the 1920s and 1930s. This view was ascribed in order to be criticized in mainstream American mass communication research as a simplistic overreaction—people are not that passive, later researchers argued, and messages are not injected directly into their minds.

An alternative model was developed, in which media influence was mitigated by social patterns—media messages involved a "two-step flow" from the media to "opinion leaders" whose views and responses helped others shape their beliefs. Much of this research was oriented toward voting behavior and public opinion, but it served to defuse the most disturbing image of media effects—direct injection of messages to a vulnerable victim.

This defusion was aided by a more psychologically oriented strain of research, focusing on the "uses and gratifications" of media by audiences. In this type of academic research, individuals were seen as being motivated by particular needs or desires, which they actively "met" via particular patterns of media behavior. Thus media use was not some addiction, but a free choice to dispel anxiety, seek diversion, or learn more about the world. An audience member was portrayed as freely choosing media use from a range of other wholesome modern activities, and as actively and rationally participating in his or her own psychic health.

The two-step flow model of media influence, and the subsequent uses and gratifications research tradition, have since been criticized, not only for their reliance on reductionist operational definitions (Carey & Kreiling, 1974), but also for their implicit celebration of "liberal pluralism." In arguing for media uses and gratifications at an individual level, American research has been charged with being blind to the more general, ideological influences of media on society.

Stuart Hall (1982), a British media scholar, has charged that mainstream American mass communication research celebrates a naive notion of freedom of choice. He argues that the "choice" being offered media audiences is a constrained, truncated choice, one that is ideologically positioned in ways congruent with capitalism, and having little to do with true democracy. By "proving" that people are influenced by opinion leaders, or by innate psychological "needs," mainstream American research ignores the general ideological context that defines what opinion leaders can and will think, and what "needs" are to be legitimated.

Thus, according to Hall and other critical scholars, "opinion" about political candidates is a forced-choice situation, and does not ever ask the deeper, underlying questions about how these candidates (products) are selected for our preferences and if, indeed, they will serve the goals and purposes they claim for themselves. Research that describes how choices are made is "administrative research," primarily serving the interests of advertisers and programmers.

The ideological processes that determine political candidates as well as products are hidden, argue critical scholars. Media influence, for Hall and for neo-Marxist scholars in general, is not in overt "messages" but in the ideological structuring of values and belief that shape or constrain the message. Ideology is evidenced in the taken for granted, the assumed, the "common sense" of a situation; it is what is not said, because it "goes without saying." It works by excluding what cannot be imagined or thought because it seems too bizarre or absurd or beyond the pale.

Notice how the idea of "hidden" or "unconscious" meanings reappears in media scholarship through the critique of mainstream or "administrative" communication research. The viewer may believe him- or herself to be conscious and alert to the persuasive blandishments of media messages, but he or she cannot be cognizant of the prestructuring that has already occurred. The media are, in this view, ideological state apparatuses, offering apparently objective, balanced, and/or merely diversionary fare, but in fact offering an elaborated form of propaganda for the status quo.

The image of the media as ideological state apparatuses is particularly important in international settings, where American media fare has tended to dominate developing nations. The fear is that people in the Third World are being educated, by this content, to become capitalist consumers. Their own traditional social and cultural mores are being eclipsed by commercial American values embedded in media fare. This is cultural imperialism, an attempt to educate and thus transform Third World nations into passive and dependent outposts of American cultural values. The education metaphor, based in notions of the media as cultivating particular kinds of values, underlies much of national as well as international criticism of media influence.

Summary

The image of the media as educational institution engages a specific set of assumptions about media/audience interactions. The assumptions are indirectly referenced in the metaphors of art and of information, when the issue of "influence on us" is addressed. The key concern, under the education metaphor, is "who we become" when exposed to mass communication.

"Education" has at least as complex and contradictory a location as "the mass media" in American social thought. Both institutions serve as touchstones for unresolved hopes and fears, and thus there are parallel charges, and tensions, in the criticism of both. Thus the contradiction between ritual and transmission views of communication appears also in education, supporting a tension between views of education as socialization (the creation and maintenance of group life) and knowledge acquisition (the absorption of a body of necessary information).

Popular criticism using this metaphor is dominated by a deeply disturbing image of a television-induced vegetative torpor, with children seen as being especially vulnerable to the hypnotic power of an addictive medium. But audiences in general are seen as being shaped by what they watch and listen to—this is especially true of "others," since the critics themselves are able to recognize, and thus escape, the dangers and risks of media exposure.

In mass communication research, the "direct effects" model was repudiated in favor of other models of socially oriented primary groups, face-to-face communication with opinion leaders, and psychologically active and motivated individuals. These models have dominated American mass communication research, but have been criticized as "administrative," as serving the interests of the status quo, because they do not question the larger, deeper, more dangerous consequences of media use.[9] The charge is that they ignore the overarching ideological influence of all media content—to support those in power, to delegitimate alternatives, to cultivate us as passive, willing, even eager consumers of political as well as commercial goods.

Thus audience members are again being seen as unwittingly transformed, this time via ideological processes. Media influence is less obvious, because ideology works through implicit structuring rather than explicit messages, but its influence is still pernicious. In current critical media theory, the media educate viewers to become unquestioning participants in a commercially motivated system, so the media directly affect who we are and who we become, even if these effects are now being imagined in more subtle and nuanced ways.

Conclusions

As we have seen, different metaphors for the media mobilize different beliefs, images, and concerns about the role of the media in contemporary life. While these three metaphors certainly do not exhaust the perspectives employed in media criticism, they do delineate some major threads in the American terrain, in popular writing, scholarly criticism, and media research.

What we have shown is that where you start determines, to a large extent, how you get to where you end up. Critics who begin with an image of the media as an unworthy art mobilize different concerns than do those who begin with the image of the media as inadequate information. Both may end up with the issue of education—who we become under the influence of the mass media—but notions of education are deeply split, in ways that parallel, but exceed, the differences between positing media as art and the media as information.

I have developed these metaphors at some length for a number of reasons. They serve first to ground and complexify the arguments delineated in Chapter 1. We can see that Macdonald, Boorstin, Ewen, and Postman draw on metaphors that are more widely and generally available in American social criticism. While each develops his own argument in his own way, each also makes use of a wider field of assumptions about the media, communication in general, human nature, and the social order. My goal was to map this wider field of assumptions about the media and mass communication in order to connect it to assumptions about human nature and the social order.

I have also attempted to show the permeability among groups of critics—the charges made by popular and by scholarly critics are not dramatically distinct from those being made by mass communication researchers and theorists. The American climate of opinion about media influence is shaped by belief and conjecture; there is no reliable tradition of scientific "findings" that can support or refute the critics' claims.

The goal here is not to decide which, if any, of the charges of media influence is "right." The first objective was to map the complex terrain of media discourse, and recognize its underlying premises and assumptions, in order to draw out its contradictions. The next step is to figure out why these particular charges, so diverse, so devastating, so complex and contradictory, are being made at all. We return to the general terrain of media/modernity discourse to explore its narrative characteristics.

Notes

1. Aesthetically oriented analyses that consider television as popular art include Newcomb's (1974) seminal book as well as various essays in *Television: The Critical View* (Newcomb, 1987). Thorburn's (1988) essay "Television as an Aesthetic Medium" clearly limns this terrain.
2. Every two years, the National Endowment for the Humanities is required, by the U.S. Congress, to issue a report on the state of the humanities in the nation. The 1988 report, written by Lynne V. Cheney, NEH chairman, is the first. The report was organized to consider the humanities in relation to colleges and universities, television, and humanities-oriented institutions such as historical societies, libraries, museums, and state councils.
3. See Stow Pearson's *The Decline of American Gentility* (1973) for an excellent discussion of the ways in which American manners are connected to social and cultural shifts and ambivalences in the nineteenth century.
4. See, for example, Rourke (1942), Mumford (1926), Croly (1909), and Brooks (1915). Kowenhoven (1949) perceptively discusses a creative American vernacular in relation to European influence.
5. It is worth noting here that traditional Marxist perspectives assume, as do logical positivist approaches, that there is a "reality" out there ("social reality") that can be deciphered. A key difference is whether that reality is veiled (false consciousness or, sometimes, ideology) or inaccessible except by special procedures (the scientific method). In some cases, theory becomes

the special procedure that allows ideology to be vanquished, giving access to "social reality."

6. See the introductory essay "The Interpretive Turn," in Rabinow and Sullivan (1979). Rorty's (1982) essay "Method, Social Science and Social Hope" is a particularly graceful discussion of these issues.

7. See Bledstein (1976) and Haskell (1977) on the ways in which professionalization and expertise emerged and shaped turn-of-the-century American life.

8. There is a fascinating heritage of self-making in American thought. An overview would include Benjamin Franklin's *Autobiography*; Emerson's essays, particularly "Self-Reliance"; the success literature increasingly popular in the nineteenth century, discussed ably by Cawelti (1965); and the copious versions of mind cure, including works by Dresser (1907), Fletcher (1895), and Trine (1897), the characteristics of which are discussed in Meyer (1980) and Parker (1973).

9. An introduction to these concerns can be found in "Ferment in the Field," the summer 1983 issue of *Journal of Communication*.

4

Characteristics of Media Discourse

Media discourse relies on a myth of seduction. Its narrative strategy parallels the stories of the Garden of Eden and of the Lorelei. These stories involve the transgression of boundaries by people in the thrall of duplicitous communication, with disastrous results. As we have seen, this vision of seduction and transgression implicitly animates much of the American criticism of the mass media.

The story of the Garden of Eden tells how a pure sphere is penetrated by the serpent, who seduces Eve into desiring the apple, which, once bitten, corrupts her, and banishes Adam and Eve from the Garden forever. The myth of the Lorelei tells of monsters disguised as beautiful maidens; their tantalizing song draws sailors off their course, onto the rocky coast, to their doom. These stories tell of corrupted innocence, of misplaced trust, of the loss of security via seduction. The voice of the snake and the song of the sirens represent temptation—the temptation to transgress boundaries.

The power of these stories depends on the existence, and recognition of, boundaries between good and evil, between truth and illusion, between wisdom and foolishness. As such, they retain connections to the metaphors of art, information, and education. Art represents the "good" in an evil world, information represents the "truth" in an illusory world, education fosters "wisdom" in a foolish world. Yet what the stories tell is that the good is always threatened by evil, the truth by illusion, wisdom by foolishness. The boundaries between these spheres are always at risk.

The narrative key to these mythic stories, then, is the notion of boundaries, of lines of demarcation. As long as clear distinctions are maintained between good and evil, truth and illusion, wisdom and foolishness, all is well. What is frightening in the stories of the Garden of Eden and of the Lorelei is that the distinctions break down. When the serpent pretends to be the voice of God, and the Lorelei pretend to be beautiful maidens, then weak, vulnerable human beings unwittingly choose their own corruption, and their doom.

In the narrative structure of the myth that informs media discourse, the media become the serpent, or the sirens. The belief is that the media can and will seduce the audience, because the media can and will blur the distinctions between good and evil, truth and illusion, wisdom and foolishness.

The media appear to be friendly, concerned, interested, understanding—like the serpent and the siren, the critics suggest, they insinuate themselves into our trust. Yet (the critics believe) the media are self-interested and duplicitous. The media seek to corrupt us so that they can control us, so that they can turn us into what they need us to be. Like Eve, we are too trusting, and perhaps already a bit corrupt; like the sailors, we are too easily drawn to appearances, and too ready to stray off course.

Thus the underlying myth of media influence encompasses the ideas of boundaries and of the consequences of transgression of those boundaries. It reproduces a familiar mythic structure, placing the media in the position of seducer or temptress, luring us into mistaking evil for good and illusion for truth, turning us away from wisdom toward foolish and, ultimately, devastating choices.

Media discourse is a social narrative, a coherent web of widely believed working assumptions about characteristics and consequences. This web is rarely made explicit or made available for test or refutation. Instead, it is mobilized to validate related social narratives. The discourse of modernity shares the seduction myth with the media discourse. Thus the two discourses seem to confirm the story of the seductive influence of media over time.

I have been suggesting that there are tensions and contradictions in these discourses that are obscured by the narrative of seduction. The media/modernity discourse is so convincing because it appears to make sense of a host of tensions and contradictions that remain unresolved in American cultural, political, social, and economic thought.

Essential Worth

We have seen how, in media discourse, art and information are deemed "essential" in a dual sense—as crucial for the creation and maintenance of a worthwhile life, and as objects having an inner substance, an intrinsic nature. Art and information are both deemed important, valuable forms that have inherent worth. They both exist "out there" in the world, available for our apprehension.

Art is characterized as being uplifting—it gives higher, more spiritual meaning to a basically material life. The vernacular conception of art, mobilized in media criticism, divides material and spiritual, and gives art the power of bestowing meaning and value onto everyday events.

The vernacular conception of information is that it gives necessary knowledge—it tells us about an outside world that we cannot "know" from firsthand experience. The more knowledge we can accumulate, the better able we are to make decisions about the world. Knowledge is gained via neutral, dispassionate information, transmitted to us undistorted by subjectivity.

Both information and art are seen as redemptive, but for different reasons. Art redeems us from a crass, materialistic world, one that is becoming increasingly mechanized and dehumanized. Information, on the other hand, redeems us from an illusory, emotionally volatile world, one that is created by our partial, subjective experience. Without art, life would be boring and driven. Without information, life would be chaotic and impulsive.

The distinctions between art and information also involve implied distinctions among reason, emotion, and aesthetic ability. A vernacular cognitive theory that underlies the narrative of seduction is one that sees the individual as basically emotional and therefore irrational, but able (with exposure to adequate information) to make important decisions. Men and women are perceived as untutored and therefore uncultivated, but able (with exposure to good culture) to make refined aesthetic discriminations.

Aesthetic ability is, it seems, the perfect blending of reason with emotion—it allows for emotive responsiveness, but in relation to worthy (because complex, demanding, "deep") cultural forms. To prefer crude, sensational entertainment to "high culture" is to betray the triumph of base emotion over higher reason. To prefer crude, sensational tabloid coverage to "real" news is to do the same. Choosing the apparently simple, accessible, crude, vulgar, titillating, distracting, and banal reveals that one has not developed the discrimination necessary to choose "good" art and "good" information.

These assumptions about discriminatory ability rest on an implicit view of human beings as requiring some form of education to become worthy. We require information to make fully rational decisions—without information we will make impulsive, selfish, "bad" decisions. We require exposure to complex, demanding, worthwhile culture—without this exposure we will make crude, base, sensationalistic choices.

In this perspective, when we are exposed to information and culture that is "bad"—simplistic or sensationalized—it appeals to us. Like junk food, we "instinctively" choose it over healthful, less immediately appealing fare. Trite, trivial, ersatz information and culture are popular because they appeal to the lowest common denominator in all of us.

Lowest Common Denominator?

The notion of the "lowest common denominator" is a perennially invoked, and rarely questioned, concept in media discourse. That the media seek to appeal to the "lowest common denominator" in the audience is invariably offered as a rebuke. It implies that media content is constructed in order to appeal to that which is lowest, basest, most "common" in the audience.

Once analyzed, this is a breathtakingly revealing construction. It assumes that each of us is a triangle, with varying degrees of "reason" or "taste" at our uppermost tips. Our "lowest" characteristic, which we share with our fellows, is our predilection for crude, violent, simplistic, sensationalistic, and/or shallow symbolic forms. Our "higher" characteristics— our intelligence, our reason, our aesthetic cultivation—are not nearly as widely shared. They are "on top" of the equation, with some of us, as Shils (1971) claims, more fully endowed than others with an ability to offset our animal passions.

Yet, one could argue that what we have in common is not "low" or "base," but sublime and wonderful. One could suggest that the media offerings that have widest appeal are in fact the ones that most speak to our humanness, our shared values and beliefs, our most treasured commonalities. From this one could argue that the most popular genres of entertainment and news are the most worthy, because they most effectively engage that which is important to the most people.

Even critics from the Left, who want most to speak for "the people," do not make this claim. The implicit belief that we are, at "base," crude and animalistic, overlaid with a fragile, in-need-of-bolstering ability to think, reason, discriminate, and evaluate, seems to prevail in criticism across the political spectrum. Our vulnerability to outside temptation is a given in the narrative. This belief is a strong challenge to the libertarian heritage of American democracy, and suggests a crucial fault line in vernacular social theory.

Egalitarian Elitism

In our discussions of how the metaphors of art, information, and education have been deployed in media criticism, we have seen how "the people" are defined somewhat paradoxically. On the one hand, they are "naturally" good and worthy, able to know and understand and discriminate until they fall under the spell of the media. This view often informs the charges from the Left, and suggests a view of the audience as innately capable, but deformed or deflected by outside influences. This view is congruent with classical libertarian theory.

At the same time, "the people" are "naturally" attracted to base, cruel, sensationalized forms, because the "lowest common denominator" in the public is passionate and animalistic. They could become more discriminating, if they are exposed to the better forms of culture. The media, in fact, could give them the kind of information and culture that would "improve" them. This is the more liberal or progressive perspective, and the one that informs the social responsibility theory of the press.

And finally, there is the position that "the people" are unevenly endowed with the top integer (intellectual acuity, sensitivity) and thus some will choose more worthy forms and others less worthy forms, and thus mass media are for the masses. The arts and the best kinds of news are to be protected from media influence, to remain pure and unadulterated for "we happy few" who can appreciate them. This is, one could argue, the conservative position, although it can be reached, as in Macdonald's case, from other points in the political spectrum.

The notion of uneven endowment, of some people simply being intrinsically more able to recognize and appreciate "the good stuff," is discomfiting under the egalitarian aegis of American culture. If cultural forms, including news, are to be seen as hierarchically organized, then it seems somehow un-American to assume that "the people" are, too. It is far more comfortable to blame the media for either turning the people into crass barbarians or failing to uplift them from their crass, barbaric state.

As we have seen, both claims are made, often by the same critics, even though they rest on very different assumptions about human nature and media influence. But these contradictory premises are made invisible under the relieving spirit of retrieved populism. The more powers that are ascribed to the media, the less necessary it is to blame "the people" for what the critic finds so deplorable. *By assuming that something called "the media" has the power to pollute the pure and/or sanctify the impure, the critic can retain faith in his or her own superior judgment while maintaining a semblance of solidarity with "the people."*

This American desire to be a populist with elitist taste is what the compromise of the ideal "democratic culture" was all about. It is also, perhaps, why the idea of news as dispassionate information is so energetically defended. If news becomes neutral facts about the world, these "facts" can be universally distributed, become available to everyone. The experts will not monopolize the knowledge, but will share it with "the people" via the organ of democracy, journalism. Everyone can join together in making public policy if this value-free information is widely available.

This view equates information, knowledge, and wisdom, holding out a possibility of full and eager participation by informed citizens in public affairs. This is a charged vision in American life, and is invoked to counter the persistent, but antidemocratic, vision of "the crowd" or "the mob." With adequate information, an informed and therefore trustworthy public is assured, and a totalitarian society deflected.

The informed public is rational and reliable, dispassionate and discriminating. The rabble is irrational and unpredictable, passionate and indiscriminate. Information can maintain a public that can be trusted. Lies, distortions, illusions—propaganda—can turn a public into a mob, a crowd that cannot be trusted. A republic ruled by the people cannot afford such a turn of events. Again, the contradiction between a naturally good (but media-deformed) versus a naturally bad (but media-salvageable) people is papered over in the call for "better media fare" that will give us "better citizens" to maintain a "better society."

The Contamination Theme

The theme that gives the seduction myth its power is the notion of contamination. Contamination involves the pollution of the previously pure, and relies on making and maintaining distinctiveness. The previous discussion has shown a number of distinctions that have been made; we now address how the processes of boundedness operate in the media/modernity story.

Under the metaphor of art, we saw that distinctions were made between art and life, between emotion and reason, between spiritual and material, between higher and lower faculties, between art and trash, between art and commerce.

Under the metaphor of information, we recognized the differences between ritual and transmission views of communication, and the epistemological distinctions that underlie these two views. We also saw that distinctions were made between perceptions and the real world, between objectivity and subjectivity, between facts and values, between news and entertainment, and between information and propaganda, and that the distinctions between emotion and reason paralleled those made under the metaphor of art.

Under the metaphor of education, we found a similar bifurcated pattern, an implicit tension between a ritual and transmission view of education, as well as assumptions about the differences between conscious and unconscious influence, between protected and unprotected media exposure, between passive and active interpretation, and between immanent and transcendent critical stances.

The mass media are seen as somehow blurring or collapsing these crucial distinctions in the world "out there," as they somehow cultivate us as the "worst" of human possibilities.

Blurring Boundaries

This opposition of spiritual and material is most obviously manifested, in American social and cultural thought, in the presumed opposition of art and commerce. Like the opposition of reason and emotion, this opposition can be connected to historical refigurations of vernacular beliefs. The industrial revolution can be seen as precipitating a refiguration of both art and commerce, just as social Darwinism and the development of physiological and behavioral sciences can be said to have precipitated a refiguration of both reason and emotion.

These refigurations are incomplete and contradictory. Vernacular values do not suddenly and completely shift; what we find instead is the grafting of partially compatible assumptions onto previous beliefs, the absorption and popularization of only some aspects of contemporary intellectual currents, the retention of older language to refer to newer constructs.

The vernacular distinctions between art and commerce, and between reason and emotion, are evidenced in social and cultural criticism in the nineteenth and twentieth centuries. These boundaries are intensely defended, perhaps because they are perceived to be most under threat. As we have seen, beliefs seem to be most vociferously defended when they are most under siege. In the intense defense of these entities as separate, and necessarily distinct, spheres, we can assume an unacknowledged recognition of their interpenetration. The vehemence of the insistence that they remain separate, bounded spheres suggests that a deeper belief in the power of order over chaos is being mobilized.

The Pure and the Polluting

Anthropologist Mary Douglas (1966/1978) has discussed the ways in which pollution beliefs operate in the social order. She suggests that "rituals of purity and impurity create unity in experience" (p. 2) and that "ideas about separating, purifying, demarcating and punishing transgressions have as their main function to impose system on an inherently untidy experience" (p. 4). She maintains, then, that a general human impulse to distinguish between the pure and the impure, and to delineate the difference and maintain the distinctions, is how we make order out of chaos—demarcations give unity and system to disjointed experience.

Douglas examines primitive (what she calls "undifferentiated") and modern ("differentiated") society, and finds purity rituals in both. While her main goal is to rescue comparative anthropology from the influence of Frazer and his notions of magic as "primitive religion," her analysis describes a general human process of separating spheres and engaging in particular ritualistic behaviors to prevent and/or punish transgression. Beliefs in "defilement" and "abominations" testify to the passionate response to transgressions—"pollution" is a danger that is constantly and actively guarded against.

We can use Douglas's notions to consider how reason and emotion, and art and commerce, are constituted as separate spheres in American thought. We can consider how the "tainting" of reason by emotion, and of art by commerce, suggests that reason and art are deemed the "pure" spheres, while emotion and commerce become the "polluting" influence.

Reason/Emotion

The distinction between reason and emotion is most obviously a heritage of the Enlightenment. The faith in the liberating powers of reason is a fundamental characteristic of classical liberal thought, and is tightly woven into the founding documents of the United States. The mistrust of emotion can be seen in Calvinism, and in the developing patriarchal definitions of men as rational and women as irrational in the nineteenth century.

Faith that man was automatically gifted with reason by God comes under siege in the nineteenth century, first through social Darwinism, then through claims by physiologists and psychologists. If man is an evolved animal, then he is also prey to the "animalistic emotions" of his origins. As Darwin (1872/ 1979) demonstrates, emotions are displayed by humans in ways hauntingly similar to those of the lower animals. "Reason" becomes, then, the key way to distinguish man from animal ancestors, and to transform these "animal instincts" into civilized, humane impulses. Reason becomes refigured—it is no longer a God-given ability, to be exercised freely, without constraints, but becomes instead a way to channel and control emotion, to overcome the instinctual passions man is born with.

By the turn of the century, physiologists and psychologists are seeking new definitions of the relationships among mind, brain, body, and experiences. The positing of "reflex arcs," as well as of an unconscious, radically refigures the previous faith in reason emerging "naturally." Reason becomes that-which-is-not-instinct, meaning both learning and the "superego," which keep the impulsive, irrational id (instincts) in check.

Apparently, then, nineteenth-century developments refigure the relationship between reason and emotion as one of "control"—the animal passions are constantly burning and churning, seeking outlet; reason must tame, soothe, deflect, and order these passions. Reason is pure, and emotion is the pollutant. The frightening consequences of emotion unchecked by reason are evidenced in the Frankenstein myth, the story of Dr. Jekyll and Mr. Hyde, violent mental illnesses, crowd behavior in revolutions—these instances of "chaos" attest to the necessity of control of emotion via reason if civilization is to survive.

The refiguring results in a strengthening, rather than a questioning, of a necessary distinction between emotion and reason. Reason becomes that-which-is-human, a trait fully developed in civilized people and only marginally evident in primitive peoples. Reason becomes the superego, that which guards against the infantile, unreasonable demands of the id.

Reason comes to be counted on as order that counteracts the corrosion of chaos; as such, it must remain separate and distinct to retain its organizing power. What is being protected, it seems, is a belief in the redemptive power of reason over emotion—if reason remains unpolluted, it can save us from the ravages of emotional response.

Art/Commerce

The distinction between art and commerce is insisted on during the rise of a commercial literary marketplace in America in the late nineteenth century. During this time, an indigenous popular mass literature is emerging, especially in magazines and novels. This is a literature that is widely popular and therefore lucrative; it attracts writers who are dismissed as "hack" writers by "real" authors and by journalists.

"Real" authors are sanctified by their connections to Art, while journalists are sanctified by their connection to Truth.[1] By declaring allegiance to a "higher good" than profit, both groups are able to distinguish themselves as honorable and to denigrate commercially successful writers as dishonorable. To write merely for money is to profane a sacred calling—in the service of either the Muse or the People.

What we see, again, is that the distinction is of most concern when it is most under threat—at stake in the late nineteenth century is the redemptive power of art over commerce. Art is deemed to represent the sacred sphere of spirit, where that which is most sublime in humankind can find expression. Commerce is deemed the crass sphere of the material, where that which is most profane in humankind can find expression. In this opposition, the profit-making activities of most Americans can be seen as a necessary but unworthy evil, an evil that deflects us from the higher, better goals of art. Art is pure, commerce is polluting.

When commerce is perceived to permeate American life, to determine increasingly the values and morals of the country, it is defined as an alienating and dehumanizing form of social intercourse, one that fosters competition, envy, deceit, trickery. Its countervailing force, art, is seen as a unifying and humanizing form, one that fosters spontaneous communal feeling.

For art to have the power to countermand commerce, it must remain pure. Commerce may be a corrupt, even a malign, force, but it is "necessary," in that society must have material processes. But commerce unleashed, without the mitigating influence of art, is dangerous, because nothing is available to counteract its ability to taint social and spiritual relations.

We can see this notion of pure and polluting spheres in the nineteenth-century distinctions between the home and the business world. As Ann Douglas (1977) argues, in the mid- to late nineteenth century, the home became defined as a sacred, spiritual site, presided over by the woman. The home was seen as a refuge from the crass, commercial competition of the business world, where men risked losing sight of deeper moral values. With the guidance and comfort of spirit-infused women, men could keep their bearings in a materialistic, competitive world.

Media Minglings

By the mid-nineteenth century, the boundaries between the material outside world and the spiritual world of the home, between the profane and the sacred, were perceived as being eroded by the mass media. First in the form of newspapers, but later in magazines, radio, and television, the mass media were bringing commercial values into the home and mixing emotional appeals with rational arguments.

The media, by their nature, seemed to appeal to emotion over reason, and to mix art with commerce. The popularity of "sensational" journalism, pulp fiction, slapstick comedy, and sentimental morality plays ostensibly attested to the power of the emotions to swamp reason and for market considerations to determine content.

The ideal dispassionate form of communication, celebrated in objective journalism, was seen as being threatened by the commercially successful, emotional forms of passionate attachment, widely offered via the mass media. These "sensational" media seemed to threaten to displace reason by pandering to emotion, thus putting at risk the presumedly fragile ability of people to control their emotions via reason.

Similarly, the "entertainment" media seemed loyal only to audience popularity (and therefore profit), rather than to the traditional virtues of high culture. Art, as represented by European forms or by particular spokesmen for an ideal democratic culture, was eclipsed by the new, seemingly crass and sensationalistic forms being purveyed by the money-hungry mass media. If art was not being eclipsed, it was being "popularized" and transformed to appeal to mass taste, thus becoming "diluted" and "homogenized." Interest in profit was determining creative expression, and thus sacred art was becoming polluted by profane commerce in the mass media.

To summarize, the media, representing the commercialization of art and the emotionalization of reason, crossed and blurred the defined boundaries between pure and impure. By doing so, the media seemed to threaten the ability of reason to control emotion, as well as the power of art to redeem us from commerce.

The catastrophic consequences of this mingling rarely exceed the bounds of the narrative structure of the seduction myth. It is enough that there has been transgression, and therefore pollution. Doom is bound to follow. As Macdonald, Boorstin, Ewen, and Postman suggest, the danger is the transgression itself. The catastrophe is the blurring of boundaries.

The worst media influence that these critics can claim is that we cannot tell art from trash, truth from illusion, persuasion from information, logic from silliness. Our perceptions have been permanently defiled, we are no longer able to distinguish the legitimate from the ersatz. The media bear the primary responsibility for this deformation of consciousness—they are the reason we can no longer perceive the necessary, and valuable, distinctiveness of these spheres.

How do the media accomplish this seduction? If the media are perceived as our modern serpent or siren, how do they manage to lure us to our own destruction? What are the particular ways that the media addle our brains, curdle our wills, divest us of our ability to discriminate between what is good and what is bad for us?

While there are a number of different specific powers ascribed to the media, they fall into a few basic categories of explanation. One category is that the media technology itself is hypnotic. Thus the flickering image on the movie screen, the throb of rock music, the light waves of the TV somehow change our consciousness and make us suggestible. Another explanatory category is that media participation involves trust and passivity: We are lulled into acquiescence because we trust we are being "taken care of" by our favorite media form.

But the most widespread explanations of how the media seduce us focus on media content rather than on the technology of delivery or the conditions of reception. These explanations will suggest, first, that media content, unlike other cultural forms, is designed to be seductive. This explanation claims that the purpose of media is to deceive us. Thus advertising is designed to trick us into buying products we do not need, while entertainment is designed to keep us watching and listening when we have other things we would rather be doing. In this criticism, the media are *by nature* sirens, luring us into a pathetic affection for what they appear to be.

A similar but distinct critique of media content is that, because it blurs the distinctions among advertising, entertainment, and news, it makes us unable to distinguish among them. Since the mass media do not reliably distinguish between fact and fiction, truth and illusion, they prevent us from being able to do so. This is seeing the media less as alluring sirens and more as misleading snakes.

If we examine these claims of the seductive power of media content, especially in relation to the notion of blurred boundaries, we find the theme of transgression and pollution at every turn. The media are seen to be both corrupt and corrupting, and the narrative cannot proceed past that assumption. It circles back on itself, and defines us as victims of an external seductive power that we cannot recognize, and thus cannot escape.

Corruption and Deflection

A characteristic of social narratives is that they involve seamlessness in logic. In this case, media criticism moves from individual to social influence without missing a beat. What is assumed to be true about the effects of the media on individuals is generalized to be true of society at large, over time. The reverse is also true. What is assumed to be writ large in social influence—pollution, blurring, corruption—is believed to be writ small in individual influence, especially on children.

Thus, just as the media are seen as "polluting" the minds of innocent, trusting viewers, by blurring reality and illusion, news and entertainment, art and commerce, reason and emotion, they are seen as having already polluted the social spirit of the nation, and thus as corrupting the purity of the past and preventing the development of a more virtuous future.

In the seamless, unsubstantiated leap from individual effects to social influence to historical trajectory, the narrative strategy remains the same—there has been a media-induced decline in American life. In the nostalgic turn, this decline is due to the loss of previous purity (the Eden myth); in the paranoid turn, this decline is due to seduction "off course" (the Lorelei myth). In either version, the media are blamed for both the *corruption* of previous innocence and the *deflection* from a previous path.

Stories of the corruption of innocence have a particular resonance in the American context. As Leo Marx (1964) argues, the story of America is the story of a despoiled Garden, a vale of purity that has been defiled by the Machine. The story of America can also be told, as we have seen, as the story of modernity, both corrupted and unredeemed by the media.

This narrative of media-based corruption and deflection resonates with the larger, deeper story of the corruption of the promise of American life. The pastoral "dream of felicity" represented by the unspoiled American continent is seen as having been tainted, eroded, transfigured by "progress," evidenced in the mechanical and artificial world of technology.

Such progress may have initially been welcomed, even eagerly pursued, but now, social critics believe, it has resulted in our downfall. Our retelling of American history suggests that we have been seduced into selling out our birthright through a misplaced faith in technology's salvational powers. Somehow, we have been misled into despoiling our virgin land.

In this retelling, the siren song of the media, like the sibilant seductions of the snake, can easily stand in for the allure of modernity, the promise of progress. The media, like modernity, apparently offer riches, leisure, ease, comfort, power. But, both media and modernity critics argue, those rewards have come at a cost. The cost is that we have gained a kingdom but lost our souls—we have the style, the aura, the illusions of mediated modernity, but we have lost the substance, the essence, the true promise of American life.

The notion of cultural decline is a crucial aspect of the critique of modernity. Modern life is seen by social critics to be a form of decadence, a loss of previous felicity, a pollution of previous potential. In spite of the marked gains in material well-being, modernity has brought with it, the critics argue, a concomitant loss of our spiritual welfare.

As we have seen, the mass media serve as scapegoats in this critique of modernity. They are deemed bearers of the corruption, and causes of the deflection, of American modernity. The media are seen as embodying all that is tainted in life, offering it to us in a seductive package, thus insinuating into us a desire for our own destruction.

The previous discussion has demonstrated how we tell the story of both media and modernity as a story of seduction, transgression, pollution, and doom. We need to consider the consequences of such a telling—what does this particular discourse make possible, and what does it make difficult? It has also been suggested that the media are blamed for all the ills of modern life. In the final chapter, the consequences of telling the story of media and modernity in these particular ways will be addressed.

Note

1. These ideas are developed more fully in my "Writing with a Machine: Typewriting and the Literary Marketplace at the Turn of the Century" (Jensen, 1987). See also Fishkin (1985) and Wilson (1985).

5

Recognitions and Reconceptualizations

How we tell our stories matters, because how we tell ourselves about our current situation determines how we act in the present, and toward the future. Our common life is shaped by the beliefs and values in our social narratives, which then become enacted in social choice, embodied in social policy, and enduring in social reforms.

The stories we tell about the mass media are crucial aspects of our common life. In these stories about media and modernity we have found gaps, elisions, contradictions, and fault lines. The media/modernity story, when closely examined, has a makeshift quality. It has been patched together to "make sense," and it offers seemingly easy ways to cure whatever ails us.

The story of media/modernity is a story that reassures because it places blame outside ourselves. It offers an attainable and nonthreatening cure—media reform—or a smug and self-serving critique—modern despair. I find this story to be simplistic, elitist, and extraordinarily naive. As currently told, the media/modernity story can animate a shallow and undemocratic social narrative.

A goal of this book has been to critique this story, in order to make it possible for us to surpass it. To this end, I have summarized the main claims of popular and scholarly critics, demonstrated the parallel social narratives of media influence and modernity, described and located historically dominant metaphors that animate media discourse, and sketched the general characteristics of that discourse.

My hope has been that, in retelling the story of media and modernity, I have made it possible for the reader to "recognize"—to see and rethink—his or her own assumptions and beliefs. Social narratives are almost impossible to prove or to disconfirm. They always seem "right," because they are the stories that are always confirmed as just being "the way things are." But if these narratives are "re-cognized," they can then be analyzed; once analyzed, they can also be evaluated—Do they make sense? Are they just? Do they open up or close down social possibilities? A purpose of the previous chapters has been to make that analysis and evaluation possible for the reader.

I have shown, I hope, that the critical discourse on media influence, in conjunction with the critical discourse on modernity, constructs an idealized past that is ever receding. I have shown how the possibility of redemption is ever present, via ideal forms like technology, art, information, or education. Either explicitly or implicitly, these are the forms against which modern media fare is evaluated, and these are the forms that are offered as mystical solutions to the perceived failures of the present. And I have demonstrated how contemporary media discourse relies on an assumption that "the people" are either inherently corrupt or easily corruptible.

My evaluation of this narrative has, of course, suffused my analysis of it. My contention has been that the ways we currently think and talk about media influence are inadequate, and that we need to find better ways to understand and evaluate the role of mass communication in modern life. But what *are* these "better ways"? Traditionally, the concluding chapter is when the author unveils his or her own criteria, or agenda, or prescription, the shining alternative to the object he or she just spent the previous chapters tarnishing.

I will not offer final criteria, agendas, or prescriptions. I will make suggestions for alternative ways to conceptualize media, culture, and society, ways that I find to be more useful, rich, and illuminating. These are, therefore, conceptions that I believe could better serve us as the basis for social narratives. Yet I am, I hope for obvious reasons, wary of claiming these as the "right" or "best" ways to think about the media in modern life. Having spent many years reading cultural and social criticism, I am painfully aware of the essential flaw in the enterprise—critics too easily believe that the world would be a better place if everyone agreed with them.

This final chapter is a restatement of the central claims of my argument, organized around my own conceptions of the media and of modern life. The media are not, to my mind, alien technologies, but human-made forms that are designed to be of cultural significance. The media are made-to-mean, both in their form and content, as part of a more general social and cultural process of living in the world. They are not outside forces, they are not unitary in their influence, and they are not, intrinsically, corrupt or corrupting.

Similarly, I do not believe that modernity is an unnatural historical force that has swept us up in an inexorable decline or deflected a "natural" progress. Modernity is a socially constructed story, a way to describe the present in relation to the past, and, as a story and as an experience, it is inherently contradictory. Modernity can be evaluated as "good" or "bad" only in relation to assumptions about the before-modern or the after-modern, and those assumptions are, always, contingent on other assumptions. There is no solid neutral historical ground against which we can evaluate current conditions. There is only the conglomeration of social narratives that have been accumulating (told, retold, transformed, and refigured) in human societies. That conglomeration is a conversation that is ongoing, one that we participate in by virtue of our membership in society. Reading and writing books constitute merely one form of speaking in this larger, ongoing conversation.

The loss of solid ground on which to stand in order to evaluate what is going on around us is frightening. I suspect that the desire for this stable, neutral territory explains many of the tendencies of the media/modernity story. Fear of what it might mean to lose this solid ground may explain the tenacity of the story, and why it is so difficult to challenge it.

This quest for certainty is understandable, and yet I do not believe that we need the solid ground of absolute criteria in order to evaluate worth. Evaluation is a socially determined process; it is the ascription of meaning to objects and processes and ideas, and thus it, too, is cultural. The ascription of worth is a central aspect of being human, and it is always social. Evaluation is inevitably contingent on a consensual process. We do not evaluate in a vacuum, or in relation to a set of rules found in neutral nature or divine law. Instead, we evaluate in relation to other people, and in relation to the stories we tell of ways of being, thinking, and acting.

This point of view assumes that valuable social change comes not from expert voices, or more information, or uplifting art, or better education, but rather from participatory, pluralistic conversation. If we talk more about what we believe, then we must think more, and evaluate more, as we run up against our differences, the incommensurability of worldviews, the complexities of human experience. If we can engage in conversation about conversation, we can better understand the ways we tell ourselves stories, and we can, in the same process, evaluate the stories that we have been told.

Because I believe this, the goal of this final chapter is to restate the major claims I have made so far, in order to foreground what I see as the undesirable consequences of current conceptions of media and modernity. My beliefs, as sketched above, are developed in this process, but only so that they are available for your response. Your ideas, in response to mine, then become part of a larger conversation about the relationships among media, culture, and society.

Media Power

When the media are criticized, it is always in relation to assumptions about their power to change things. The media are assumed to have the power to transform "us," the audience, and/or "good stuff," deemed art, information, or education. Media power is understood as the ability to "ruin" or "corrupt" the audience, as well as to "ruin" or "corrupt" necessary and valuable communication forms. Media power is deemed to be both psychological and cultural—working at the levels of individual perception *and* cultural quality. Thus, socially, we the audience become less worthy, while at the same time modern culture becomes less worthy.

This assumed double punch (the corruption of the culture and of the consumer) leaves almost no hope of breaking the spell. The media are seen as having a totalizing influence, because they corrupt at the level of choice as well as the level of cultural quality. Not only do they not offer the kinds of artistic, informational, and educational fare that they "should," but they have made us unable to recognize or seek out such fare, should it become available. Thus the critic can do little more than bemoan the effects of the media in modern life, in the hope that, somehow, criticism will spark therapeutic change.

This ascription of media power allows, as we have seen, an explanation for why modern life is not what it is supposed to be. Because "we" are not to blame, an ideal democratic society, run by rational and discriminating citizens, is still possible. By ascribing corrupting power to the media, we can maintain faith in a democratic social vision.

What is gained, then, is a way to support the notion of participatory democracy without relinquishing authority to the current "vulgar" tastes and choices of the people. The media critic deplores the tastes and choices being made, and yet keeps faith with an American dream of worthy choices, made by a worthy public.

What is avoided, however, is an engagement with the lived experience of everyday people. Their actual choices, preferences, and desires are defined a priori as corrupt. They need not be taken seriously because they are already media-tainted, impure manifestations of the power of the media to pollute the individual. This is a breathtakingly disrespectful attitude toward other members of contemporary society, yet it appears egalitarian because it never really blames us—instead, it blames the "unnatural" intervention of an alien force.

But is mass communication best understood as an outside, unnatural intervention? Could it not, more appropriately, be seen as a particular mode of organizing public thought and discussion? What would be the consequences of rethinking media power as cultural conversation, of rethinking the modern condition as a particular mode of social organization?

If we acknowledge the historic series of transformations in forms of communication, from oral to written to print to electronic, we acknowledge that particular forms of communication are associated with particular possibilities and limits. Oral forms tend to support small, intimate social groups, and the use of memory to locate the present in relation to the past. Writing allows the retention and storing of knowledge, but at a cost—it can be monopolized in ways that centralize power. Yet, writing, and later printing, allows the dispersion of knowledge in ways that can include previously excluded groups. Printing can "freeze" languages in ways that support larger identifications, break down some linguistic barriers while solidifying others, include more people into larger, and perhaps more liberating, perhaps more confining, collectivities.[1]

If we examine the possibilities and limitations of shifts from oral to print communication, we can ask better questions about the consequences of electronic forms. First, we can recognize that the development and diffusion of electronic forms alters, but does not eliminate, characteristics of orality and print. Transformations of communication forms occur in relation to the society and culture in which they are deployed, and never "drop from the sky," working automatic and unitary changes.

To acknowledge the tendencies of certain communication forms is to raise important questions about general influence on modes of thought and modes of social organization. Some suggest that electronic communication, because of its capacity to collapse time and space, to communicate across the globe instantaneously, creates a global village; others, in a dystopic vision, suggest an information overload.

These are simplistic conceptualizations that reproduce the naïveté of technological boosterism and fail to address the complexity of communication influence on individuals and society. Is it the capacity of the system itself that makes this transformation, or the meanings being communicated, or the ways in which they are understood and interpolated into everyday life that makes the difference? Can these be separated, and against what should they be compared?

To let go of the myth of an invasive, corruptive media power only to make totalizing statements about the "inherent" nature of oral, print, or electronic forms of communication is to replace one simplistic discourse with another. What I am suggesting is that we might better conceptualize media power as cultural connectedness. If we see the mass media as modern cultural processes, then we understand them as forms of connection among people, as ways to "tell the world" among social groups.

To understand richly the influence of changes in modes of communication, we would need to conduct careful comparative study at a variety of levels, across time. We can study and consider the developmental relationships among oral, written, printed, and electronic forms. We could then investigate the ways in which dominant modes of communication can foster, as well as deflect, certain modes of thought and forms of social life. This kind of investigation requires a letting go of the belief that the power of the media is to corrupt us and "authentic" forms of communication, and believing, instead, that the contemporary mass media offer new forms of connection that have possibilities as well as limits.

Redemptive Forms

I have shown how media discourse invokes notions of the possibility of redemption via cultural purity. The unchallenged assumption is that there are certain kinds of cultural fare that are in-and-of-themselves worthy—these are forms that are seen to have an automatically ennobling and uplifting influence on us. These are the very forms that the media are seen either as failing to offer or as virtually destroying.

What is gained in this telling of the story is the possibility of modernity's "cure" if the "right kind" of content would be disseminated via mass communication. These ideal forms offer an unspecified "goodness" that will suffuse the populace and create or restore virtue. What is avoided, in such a telling, are the complexities of evaluative consensus. Just whose good is being called for, and which virtues? Also elided is a thinking through of the relationship between cultural forms and social transformation. Magically, good stuff is invoked as a salvational process, an automatic antidote to modernity's ills. How this miracle is pulled off is never fully explored.

Thus art is defined as a form of culture that will refine and cultivate the barbaric tendencies of the masses. If it is "democratic art," it will spring from the natural worthiness of the common man, and, like all "true art," it will awaken that which is most civilized in each of us. The media do not, the critics believe, offer anything of the sort—instead they "cater to" the barbaric tendencies of the modern mass man. They homogenize or trivialize or banalize or commercialize artistic expression by appealing to the so-called lowest common denominator. The audience who watches such "trash" becomes trashy too, indulged in its naturally low tastes or seduced into accepting junk as meaningful.

Similarly, information is defined as a form of culture that will somehow make us rational and give us the tools to make wise public decisions. Information becomes the panacea for a technologically advanced democracy, because it appears to offer a neutral, participatory terrain in and through which progressive public policy can be made. Information as a reliable "picture of the world" has been an American dream since the turn of the century, when the full complexities of industrial democracy became undeniable. The mass media do not offer a reliable, neutral, or complete picture of the world, and thus are castigated for their bias, stereotyping, and omissions. "We" are being either indulged in our "natural" desire for sensationalistic news or seduced into wanting such exotic or entertaining fare by the unworthy practices of the mass media.

Finally, education is offered as the institution that assures that the citizens of tomorrow are given the knowledge, and cultivation, that "true" information and art can offer. Mass education is an attempt to do what the media are supposed to do, too—educate the populace to recognize and respond to the forms of culture that will make them civilized, refined, wise, and rational. The media do not do this, the critics claim, and education is not fully succeeding in the ways hoped for. Again, the media can become the scapegoat, since the education system "can't compete" with what is on TV and in movies, comic books, and advertisements.

The deployment of these particular metaphors is a rhetorical set-up. Certain idealized forms of culture are defined and then compared with the media. The media neither offer them in their full glory nor turn us into the kinds of people who could or would appreciate them in their most exalted forms. But what, exactly, are these wonderful ideal forms? Do they have the powers ascribed to them? Can they so readily transform the world? What would be the consequences of letting go of this magical thinking, and of reconceptualizing art, information, and education?

To discover what "art" and "information" and "education" are supposed to be, we can look to the past, seeking to discover when and where these forms were "precorrupt" and therefore at their most powerful and pure. Of course, this redemptive narrative unravels when we take a backward glance. We find that art has never been a simple or unitary expression of some untrammeled ennobling spirit, but is instead a historically grounded, socially located, contingent practice.

High art production has historically been related to systems of patronage; if we redefine art, the issue becomes not how we can free art from the evil influence of commerce, but instead, Which systems of support offer the best kinds of art for our purposes? Art production has always involved systems of legitimation, and the issue becomes, Which systems of evaluation offer the best kinds of art for our purposes? At stake, when the questions are posed in this manner, are what we call "best" art and what, in fact, "our" purposes are.

When the media are simplistically criticized as "bad art," we are less able to ask questions about how we decide what is "good" and "bad," worthy and unworthy. Unless we question *how* worth is ascribed, aesthetic value seems to be in the work itself, as a representation of a higher, "natural" aesthetic law. We avoid tough issues of social valuation if we pretend that worth is a predetermined quality discoverable in a concrete object.

Further, until we unpack the metaphors, we cannot acknowledge the complexities of ascertaining public purposes—the definitions of "us," as well as the definitions of the "public good." "We" are not a unitary, homogeneous group of people whose needs and interests will inevitably be served by the same thing, and our purposes may not be similar, or congruent.[2] The possibility of inevitable social conflict and incommensurably different social goals can be addressed once we give up a simplistic notion of art as magically and uniformly redemptive.

The critique of the media as "bad art" rests on the implicit assumption that there is a mass of people who "need" or "deserve" to be uplifted by specific forms of automatically redemptive culture. This construction is most easily questioned when its fundamental assumptions are brought to light—questions about how art is defined and what purposes are ascribed to it. As we come to question the "automatic" definition of things as artistic because they are in museums, or worthy because they are taught in schools, we can also question that audiences need particular kinds of uplift, based on the assumption that the mass audience is naturally barbaric and/or easily seduced into a barbaric state.

We can begin to unpack the patronizing belief that something called art is a necessary and valuable form of civilizing the wild self, and consider instead that various forms of culture offer various meanings, used for various purposes, often contradictory ones. We can start to look for how cultural forms operate among particular groups of people, recognizing not only the status and class purposes of some forms of art, but also the emotional, aesthetic, social, and personal meanings that various cultural practices can create and sustain among specific peoples.

We can suggest that some forms of culture are more worthy than others, but not because of the inherent textual traits they are believed to possess. Aesthetic worth is ascribed, not given, and may best be seen as an aspect of associated practice. We can ask of cultural forms—from classical music to soap operas to boxing to pornography—What kinds of actions are manifested in relation to what forms of culture?

These actions, because they are public, can be discussed in relation to the public good, and then we are led back into the complicated but crucial realm of determining public policy in a democratic society. We may never be able to escape the desire to prescribe "good beliefs and values" for groups other than ourselves, but we can at least recognize how dependent those values are on our own self-interested assumptions.

Similarly, notions of "information" and "education," as formulated in the media/modernity discourse, operate to prevent questioning of the fundamental difficulties of modern democratic life. Like art, these forms are seen as being automatically redemptive, in that they make possible a more valuable person and thus a more worthwhile society. What happens when we rethink this assumption that information and education are therapeutically transformational?

Again, the narrative tapestry unravels if we closely examine the historic development of faith in these forms as inherently redemptive. Information is seen to be, like art, a contingent practice, linked to epistemological assumptions about the decodability of the world, and a refiguring of earlier libertarian notions of the role of the press in society.

Like art, the ideal information is also connected to assumptions about the need to "civilize" or "tame" irrational tendencies: Information is supposed to foster reason and logic, while something called entertainment supposedly caters to the irrational and emotional. The ideal of news as information develops just as faith in the possibility of complete, neutral pictures of the world is being challenged. In this way, the ideal of "objective information" becomes a talisman against modernity.

Once we recognize this, we can ask better questions about how we can and should "know" the world, if something called objective information is an epistemological impossibility. Rather than simply bemoaning the "badness" of news coverage in the mass media, we can think instead about how stories of the world are told, and ask, What kinds of stories are most valuable for our purposes? Are there good or useful purposes served by different forms of news narratives? By statistics as well as by celebrity stories? By docudramas as well as by talk shows?

Again, once we challenge the logic of hypothetical ideal forms, we are thrust into explicitly considering what we mean by "valuable." Do we mean valuable for empathy? For technological decisions? For local involvement? For national unity? For individual dignity? For critical capacity? We can consider whose interests and purposes are served by current conditions of news evaluation and practice, and imagine and work toward different systems of "telling the world."

As long as we continue to reify something called information as a redemptive force and castigate the media for failing to offer it appropriately, we are caught in a self-validating critique that avoids the really difficult issues of modern public life. Once we acknowledge that worth is ascribed, not given, we can more readily question whose interests and purposes are best served by the status quo, and imagine alternative modes.

Finally, the metaphor of education incorporates both art and information as "cultivating" influences, and shows how, socially, the role of education has become institutionally established as a distinct kind of childhood practice. In the logic of the dominant discourse, an ideal cultural form, education, somehow ensures that future generations will be both cultivated and informed. Education is reified, and hopes are pinned on circumscribed institutional inculcation that cannot question the terms of its operation. Education is an automatic good, because it is deemed to transmit information and cultivate civilized selves.

But as we have seen, and as recent discussions of the curriculum indicate, education too is a historically locatable, socially grounded, and value-laden practice. Once the "automatic" or "natural" terms of evaluation are put up for questioning, then decisions about what should or should not be included in the curriculum become foregrounded. Once the canon of "good culture" is questioned, we are forced to consider how we decide what should be taught. Once the possibility of "objective information" is challenged, what body of irrefutable facts can be taught? Whose history do we teach? Whose science? For what purposes? With what hopes?

Education is a terrain where recent rethinking of cultural hierarchies and recognition of the contingent nature of inquiry are acutely manifested. At the university level, these rethinkings and recognitions appear in relation to a core curriculum, or the hopes of a common body of crucial knowledge; at the level of secondary education, in terms of the geographic and historical literacy of high school students; at the elementary level, in relation to mastery of basics of reading, writing, and arithmetic, as well as textbook descriptions of evolution and history.

In spite of this controversy over the value and purposes of mass education, there is agreement that the media are doing an even worse job than the schools. This assumption needs to be thought through, and we can do so only if we shed the assumption that the media are a corrupt form of ideal education. We can ask, instead, What is necessary or valuable knowledge? How can it be shared? Is the current system of mass education inherently the best? Are the mass media somehow challenging or eclipsing this system, or are they both aspects of some larger cultivation process?

Education, like art and information, is a concept that seems an automatic good, and yet we have seen that it is an "empty set" we fill with assumptions (often contradictory) about potential purposes. The consequences of lack of education are deemed to be the same as those of a lack of art or information—a rude, untutored, uncivilized populace.

But we can question this dominant discourse, and rethink education as the process of acculturation and socialization, as the ways in which each of us connects up with the culture and society into which we have been born. Under a different conceptualization, we can suggest that we learn our world in varieties of ways, and forms of mass communication can "tell us the world" in ways that are deemed socially valuable as well as in ways that are socially dangerous.

If we rethink "education" in this way, we are forced back into questions that are avoided in the current discourse. We can consider whose interests and purposes are being served by the present system of education, and whether there are better ways for our children, and ourselves, to engage with culture and society. What kinds of education are best? For whom? With what consequences? There are no easy answers to these questions, but they need to be confronted, not avoided, and confronted in relation to mass communication. To continue to treat the mass media as evil antagonists that seduce us away from more worthy pursuits is to avoid the difficulties of rethinking social progress.

Historical Trajectories

At its most demonic, the media/modernity discourse paints a picture of the media cultivating us as mindless drones, unable to engage in any valuable activities, our minds full of trivia, unable to tell fantasy from reality, vulnerable to the blandishments of suave politicians. This nightmare incorporates the twin specters of mass culture/mass society—the synergistic forces that are believed to destroy progressive, liberating, democratic life.

It is important, when we acknowledge the connections between fears of media influence and fears of mass society, that we respect the historical existence of totalitarian rule and the role of propaganda in creating and sustaining it. A risk in showing how the media/modernity story is simplistic and paranoid is the possibility that *all* notions of dangerous communication consequences will be dismissed.

Again, my purpose here is to suggest that there are more useful ways to conceptualize media and modernity than as the progressive disintegration, or deflection of, ideal society. A reconceptualization of media and modernity would include understanding how communication operates in political and social repression as well as in liberation, seeing communication and history as operating for as well as against democratic possibilities.

It is important to understand and respect why we have told the media/modernity story in the ways that we have. I have been suggesting that such a telling makes possible a coherent and reassuring placing of blame, and that it avoids confrontation of paradoxes and contradictions. We tell the story of media influence in ways that let us address, however incompletely, a deeper ambivalence about our collective history.

I contend that the mass media serve us as scapegoats for modernity—we blame them not only for what is wrong with modern life, but also for failing to save us from it. We see the media as causing modern evils, as well as preventing us from escaping from those evils. I believe that, until we recognize that media criticism is a displaced critique of modern life, we will continue to deflect a necessary reevaluation of the nature and characteristics of modernity.

We have seen how the critique of modernity parallels and intersects with assumptions of media influence. The critique of modernity encompasses all claims about the nature of contemporary life, in relation to what has gone before, and in relation to what could be. The modernity critique proceeds in relation to beliefs about history, contemporary reality, and future possibility. It is laden with unexamined assumptions and unresolvable contradictions; unpacking it can help us to confront these difficult tensions more directly.

There is a fundamental contradiction in all discussions of modern life; this contradiction is inevitably elided when we scapegoat the media. This contradiction is in the ways that we conceptualize tradition and modernity—the liberating consequences of the loss of tradition are also perceived as the debilitating consequences of modernity.

As the traditional bonds of community disappear, individual freedom and choice appear enhanced. But this freedom, and these choices, come at some cost. What is no longer given must be constructed anew, and the costs of this construction are, the critics believe, alienation, isolation, and anomie. The story of modernity is the story of tensions between a vision of the past as repressive but supportive and a vision of the present as liberating but alienating. How can this double duality be reconciled?

In America the hope was that, loosed from the repressive bonds of the past, "natural" communal ties would emerge. The New World would offer more authentic ways to give orientation and meaning to individual lives. Instead, a modern society emerged, one whose orientation and meaning seem, to most critics, to be specious. Modern values seem meretricious, modern tastes banal, modern actions motivated by self-interest, not altruism or decency. The modern condition, fragmented, alienated, insecure, offers little apparent possibility for the rich, meaningful life that should have emerged.

This is another enclosing narrative, a self-confirming picture of the loss of a dream. It tells a nostalgic story either of decline (from some earlier arcadia) or of lost possibility (for some unrealized utopia). The dominant discourse animates the optimism that greets each new communication form—perhaps *this* will finally make possible the ideal modern society that has been deflected. Perhaps new communication technologies will give us the perfect blend of community in society, of egalitarian elitism, of secular faith, of progress without alienation.

As redemption fails to arrive, as each new medium seems to reproduce, rather than transcend, the perceived ills of contemporary life, frustration grows. Under current conceptualizations, our only attitude toward social hope is one of mourning a lost past, or waiting for an unfolding future.

This passive stance, where we are constructed by historical forces that take us away from or toward an ideal world, is a dangerous one. It naturalizes social change, as if, like the seasons, it fluctuates beyond our control. We imagine a historical trajectory that sweeps us up, and thus must be accepted and "put up with," since it operates on its own, without our participation.

Thus we can imagine that new technologies will emerge and save us. Yet, if we examine the historical implications of technology, we see that innovation is not unidimensional in origin or influence. New or different forms of communication do not act as automatic solvents, transforming us into the ideal citizens of an ideal world. Instead, it seems that forms of communication are simply another form of modern association, ways in which we connect up with the world. They are technologically based forms of cultural participation, and thus are aspects of social life. Conceptualized in this way, the mass media, like all technologies, can be seen as historically connected to deeply cultural, and therefore deeply social, purposes.

It is easy to see technologies as "unnatural," as outside of history and society, as imposed on an ongoing culture. But technologies, including communication technologies, emerge and are deployed in relation to cultural practices and social relationships. Like all practices and relationships, they structure, and are structured by, each other. Telling the story of a unitary outside force imposed on an ongoing society prevents us from recognizing the complexities of influence and progress. It fosters not only a despairing story of corruption and loss, but also a naive hope of salvation via technological change.

Until we shed the media/modernity discourse, we will continue to avoid asking what modernity makes possible, what it prevents, who it serves, who it harms. We can let the narrative continue to absolve us from any responsibilities—something outside ourselves is to blame, and something other than ourselves may appear to fix it. We can maintain both a self-righteous cynicism and a simplistic optimism if we blame the media for modernity's ills.

Immanence as Transcendence

The discourse of media/modernity represents a very American terrain, one that is optimistic, that believes in transformation, and that invokes some version of democracy. Idealized visions of art, information, education, and technology support a vision of an inclusive, participatory society, one that can and will emerge under the right conditions. The confines and constraints of history, tradition, authority, and scarcity can be surpassed—we can be cut loose from what binds us, given the right techniques and tools.

I am arguing here that it is dangerously naive to assume that we will be saved by art, by information, by education, by technology. The implicit hopes of some media critics for redemptive symbolic forms, purveyed by some ideal communication system, reveal a chronic waiting for salvation. The media/modernity discourse, as now constructed, implicitly absolves us from active engagement in reconstructing our social world—we wait for outside forces to make things better, dramatically and permanently.

A luxurious intellectual despair also characterizes the dominant critiques of the modern condition. The assumption that modern life is fragmented and chaotic, vacuous and reduced to spectacle, anoints the critic and disparages the people who are living, working, struggling, sacrificing, and choosing within this historical moment. The critic somehow transcends the forces that suffuse the lives of everyone else.

When we blame the media, we smugly exonerate ourselves, our economic system, our social choices, our actions, and our desires—we free ourselves from blame, and place it on "it" (the media) and "them" (the unwashed masses who have no taste/have been seduced/have not had the proper cultivation). Blaming the media for causing or perpetuating evil allows critics to define an alternative ideal world, one in which everyone would be, and act, more like them.

This ideal world is one that magically transcends the grubby reality of contemporary existence. It offers an imaginary space for harmony, beauty, truth, and wisdom. Those who dwell in it are transformed into ideal citizens of an ideal democracy. Such a society may have been possible in the past, or may be developed in the future, except, of course, for the corrupting media.

A central tenet in the critique of the media, and of modernity, is that a "natural" good is being deformed and deflected by an "artificial" outside evil. This natural good is, it seems, this idyllic, imaginary past/future. The utopian potential flavors descriptions of social change, and flavors our understanding of the role of media in it.

I mistrust this juxtaposition of a naturally evolving good with an artificial, external evil. Such a construction places too much faith in transcendence, and too little faith in immanence. It constructs a world besieged only by external sin, which must somehow be banished, or redeemed by sublime intervention. The grubby now can be changed into the pristine past/future, once that which is impure is banished, so that that which is pure is allowed free reign.

It seems to me that we are merely biologically natural—we are also richly and more interestingly cultural. All that is human-made is cultural, and thus cannot be deemed "unnatural," unless we imagine only the divine as authentic. Culture, in all its manifestations, is humanly created and sustained—it is the imagined actualized in practice, ideas made material.

To claim "the natural" as some circumscribed, basic, and redemptive set of options, and to dismiss as "artificial" all that is socially constructed, technically developed, or commercially disseminated, would be to repudiate all but the most mundane aspects of contemporary life. There is little we can point to as fundamentally "natural"—like the premodern, it unravels as it is traced back. "Naturalness," like art, education, and information, operates as an empty set that we fill with illusory guarantees of purity, goodness, or worth.

If we rethink the assumed distinctions between "natural" and "artificial," believing instead in varieties of culture, then the implications of distinctions between the "authentic" and "commercial" can be directly considered. It is more useful, I believe, for us to consider the created, the fictional, the cultural, the social, *and* the commercial as human constructions. Stories, shopping malls, factories, and social systems are all human-made, and must be judged in relation to the influences they have and the purposes to which they are put.

Consequences of Reconceptualization

But is this reconceptualization safe? What happens when we let go of the fundamental boundaries that inform the social narrative of media/modernity? The fear is that, without distinctions, our moral discussions will sink into a vicious relativism. This fear is one that has recurred in current discussions of media, culture, and society, and it is one that needs to be addressed head-on.

The idea of a relativistic moral universe is frightening. This is because it appears to be both a universe without certainty and a universe open to all kinds of cruel or vicious practices. Relativism appears to say "anything goes," and to make all actions equivalently meaningful, or meaningless. This is why literary canons, aesthetic evaluations, and distinctions between truth and fiction, authentic and commercial, real and ersatz seem so crucially necessary. Canons and distinctions appear to offer reliable anchors and bulwarks against evil in a chaotic and fluctuating world.

We have seen how each media critic seeks to protect and defend the virtuous against corruption. The media/modernity story is one of pollution, and the hope is that the good, valuable, and true will be saved from the bad, worthless, and false. This salvation depends on boundaries not being crossed, the sacred not being profaned, the separate domains remaining distinct.

I have implied that these distinctions are constructed, and believe that they should be reconstructed. This appears to challenge the very foundations of social evaluation—what is to prevent someone from purveying art as trash, advertising as education, fiction as fact, the false as the real, the cruel as the kind? Challenging the established system by which we anoint some things as worthy and others as unworthy appears to open up the possibility of rampant relativism and a world where nothing is sacred, or safe.

But recognizing the contingency of distinctions, realizing how they rest on contradictory or illogical foundations, does not banish them or open the door to all manner of viciousness and evil. Evaluation—of people, things, places, societies, the past and the future—is a cultural practice, too, and it always proceeds in relation to issues of value, which seem ultimately to rest on issues of purpose.

If we recognize the contradictory values mobilized in media discourse, we can locate those assumptions that deserve reconceptualization. Our task becomes to recognize and support those purposes we deem most worthy, individually and socially, and proscribe those we do not. If we rethink the values and beliefs that operate in the media/modernity discourse, we will not abandon or throw away all evaluative distinctions. We will, instead, more directly address how individuals and groups in a society can support and proscribe purposes in ways that are just.

The communications media were hailed as having redemptive potential in relation to a democratic dream of a free *and* just society, one where individual freedom could flourish, fairly and collectively. This dream is an inspiring one. It is the supposed route to this society that is obscure in the narrative—as now conducted, the media/modernity discourse offers only a magical route to its orienting vision of a free and just society.

The social narrative of media/modernity tells us that the media deflect the democratic dream by individually and collectively distorting our sensibilities, depriving us of free choice, and subverting rational decision making. It tells us that we are already doomed, unless we develop an antidote—the critical consciousness that somehow these critics have themselves achieved. It also tells us that we can somehow become "undistorted," achieve some imaginary state of natural grace, where we are free from the corruptions of contemporary culture.

It is important to realize, I believe, that we have never been able to surpass culture, never been able to transcend the habits, values, and beliefs into which we are born and through which we become human. What is so valuable about modernity is that it offers the possibility of recognizing and questioning aspects of the cultural web in which we are suspended. Such a recognition and questioning is the Enlightenment legacy that continues to thrive in our social thought.

This gives us the possibility of recognizing our presuppositions, and of re-cognizing, rethinking them. It means we can think about how we think, criticize how we criticize, evaluate how we evaluate. This is made possible because modernity multiplies the interpretive worlds in which we share, and thus means we have some measure of choice over how to think and how to believe.

Recognizing the Dream

The dream of an egalitarian, plural American democracy suffuses the dominant discourse of media/modernity. I deem it a worthy purpose, a valuable vision to orient and engage social hope.[3] In short, I believe it needs all the recognition and support we can muster. But a just and free society is not automatic or "natural"—that is the undeniable lesson of the past 200 years. A democratic society is culturally created and maintained, against daunting odds. If we rethink the media/modernity discourse, we can revivify our responsibility and role in the democratic project.

Social transformation does not happen autonomously, and natural good is not deflected by unnatural outside forces. To blame the media for the ills of modernity is to mistake the aspect for the cause, and to silence what could be an important and worthwhile social conversation.

The most appropriate stance toward media and modernity, is, I believe, one of respectful participation. In relation to the media, we can respect their popularity and their ubiquity, and seek to understand why they are popular and ubiquitous. We can seek to understand, from the point of view of participants, the meanings that are made in and through mass communication.

Rather than assuming that the media are invariably repressive, deforming, destructive, and evil, we can listen to those who participate in them to discover the multiple ways in which they are enjoyed and understood as well as the ways in which they are disliked and deplored. We can also seek to understand our own connection to media and society—criticism is too often conducted from a disdainful distance.

We can also learn to understand the media as aspects of contemporary culture, aspects that are not the sole determinant of our common life. We live our lives on many levels, in different ways simultaneously; we who study the media (or anything else) too often forget this in our quest to explain the world via our own expertise.

In relation to modernity, we can recognize the ease with which history is transformed into argument, the ways in which we use the past to justify our attitude toward the present. Attempts to understand the past as lived experience can be used to compare contemporary structures and habits with previous ones, recognizing always that these attempts are prey to the vagaries of our own desires to justify or condemn our contemporary situation.

We can recognize, too, the variety in modernity, and more readily celebrate the ways in which modern life offers the opportunity to critique it so roundly. If we assume, as I do, that all individuals (not just intellectuals) are able to understand and evaluate (only) some of the conditions of existence, then modern American life offers the possibility of going against as well as with the grain of modernity, of taking part and taking apart. Modernity is not a unidimensional force, but a multifaceted condition, one that offers far more possibilities than most critics allow.

Finally, many of the criticisms of modernity are complaints of abundance—anomie and alienation, however painful, are less worthy of our collective concern than are the unequal distributions of power, wealth, and resources and the humanly created injuries of class, race, and gender. Continuing to condemn the media, or modernity, as uniformly evil prevents us from separating the truly cruel from the transitorily corrosive.

Blaming the media for causing all that is wrong with modern life prevents us from recognizing the constructed interrelationship of economics, politics, and culture in the formation and maintenance of contemporary conditions. As we negotiate new terminology to acknowledge that these, too, are not distinct outside "forces," we can rethink how we construct social relations and social explanations. We can become less eager to blame an alien force for whatever ills beset us, or to believe that we can somehow "fix" the media and thus render ourselves cured. We can, at the very least, study and think about what the media are blamed for, because these are the ills that concern us. The ills for which the media are inappropriately blamed still deserve our attention, concern, and action.

In redefining the discourse on media/modernity, the mass media can become a site for collective conversation. To the extent that media content embodies modern culture, media practices reproduce social relations, and media criticism animates consideration of "what is the good," the study of the media can foster discussion of what we, as individuals and as a society, create, maintain, and desire. I am enough of an American to believe that discussion is where we begin.

Notes

1. Readings that would help support such a reconceptualization include Innis (1951, 1972), Ong (1982), and Eisenstein (1979).
2. See Isaiah Berlin's (1988) eloquent essay for a discussion of the incommensurability of human purposes.
3. My thinking on this issue has been shaped in part by Rorty's recent book, *Contingency, Irony and Solidarity* (1989).

References

Arendt, Hannah (1971). *Society and culture.* In Bernard Rosenberg & David Manning White (Eds.), *Mass culture revisited.* New York: Van Nostrand Reinhold.

Bell, Daniel (1956). The theory of mass society: A critique. *Commentary, 22,* 75-83.

Bellah, Robert N., Madsen, Richard, Sullivan, William M., Swidler, Ann, & Tipton, Steven M. (1985). *Habits of the heart: Individualism and commitment in American life.* Berkeley: University of California Press.

Bendix, Reinhard (1970). Tradition and modernity reconsidered. In Reinhard Bendix, *Embattled reason: Essays on social knowledge.* New York: Oxford University Press.

Berlin, Isaiah (1988, March 17). On the pursuit of the ideal. *New York Review of Books,* pp. 11-18.

Berman, Marshall (1970). *The politics of authenticity: Radical individualism and the emergence of modern society.* New York: Atheneum.

Bledstein, Burton J. (1976). *The culture of professionalism: The middle class and the development of higher education in America.* New York: Norton.

Bode, Carl (1965). *The half-world of American culture: A miscellany.* Carbondale: Southern Illinois University Press.

Boorstin, Daniel J. (1972). *The image: A guide to pseudo-events in America.* New York: Atheneum.

Bramson, Leon (1961). *The political context of sociology.* Princeton, NJ: Princeton University Press.

Brooks, Van Wyck (1915). *America's coming-of-age.* New York: B. W. Huebsch.

Brown, Richard D. (1976). *Modernization: The transformation of American life, 1600-1865.* New York: Hill & Wang.

Carey, James W. (1989). *Communication as culture: Essays on media and society.* Boston: Unwin Hyman

Carey, James W., & Kreiling, Albert L. (1974). Popular culture and uses and gratifications: Notes toward an accommodation. In Jay G. Blumler & Elihu Katz (Eds.), *The uses of mass communications: Current perspectives on gratifications research.* Beverly Hills, CA: Sage.

Cawelti, John G. (1965). *Apostles of the self-made man.* Chicago: University of Chicago Press.

Cheney, Lynne V. (1988). *Humanities in America: A report to the president, the Congress and the American people.* Washington, DC: National Endowment for the Humanities.

Clarke, I. F. (1979). *The pattern of expectation, 1644-2001.* London: Jonathan Cape.

Croly, Herbert (1909). *The promise of American life.* New York: Macmillan.

Curran, James, Gurevitch, Michael, & Woollacott, Janet (Eds.). (1979). *Mass communication and society.* Beverly Hills, CA: Sage.

Czitrom, Daniel J. (1982). *Media and the American mind: From Morse to McLuhan.* Chapel Hill: University of North Carolina Press.

Darwin, Charles (1979). *The expression of emotions in man and animals.* New York: St. Martin's. (Original work published 1872)

Davis, Robert E. (1976). *Response to innovation: A study of popular argument about new mass media.* New York: Arno.

de Lauretis, Teresa, Huyssen, Andreas, & Woodward, Kathleen (Eds.). (1980). *The technological imagination: Theories and fictions.* Madison, WI: Coda.

Dewey, John (1947). *The public and its problems: An essay in political inquiry.* Chicago: Gateway. (Original work published 1927)

Douglas, Ann (1977). *The feminization of American culture.* New York: Knopf.

Douglas, Mary (1978). *Purity and danger: An analysis of the concepts of pollution and taboo.* London: Routledge & Kegan Paul. (Original work published 1966)

Dresser, Horatio W. (1907). *Health and the inner life.* New York: G. P. Putnam's Sons.

Eisenstein, Elizabeth L. (1979). *The printing press as an agent of change: Communications and cultural transformations in early modern Europe.* New York: Cambridge University Press.

Ewen, Stuart (1976). *Captains of consciousness: Advertising and the social roots of the consumer culture.* New York: McGraw-Hill.

Ferment in the field. (1983). *Journal of Communication, 33*(3) [Special issue].

Fishkin, Shelley Fisher (1985). *From fact to fiction: Journalism and imaginative writing in America.* Baltimore: Johns Hopkins University Press.

Fletcher, Horace (1895). *Menticulture, or the ABC of true living.* Chicago: A. C. McClurg.

Frank, Waldo (1929). *The rediscovery of America.* New York: Charles Scribner's Sons.

Frank, Waldo (1937). *In the American jungle.* New York: Farrar & Rinehart.

Franklin, Benjamin (1986). *Benjamin Franklin's autobiography: An authoritative text, background, criticism.* New York: Norton.

Gans, Herbert J. (1974). *Popular culture and high culture: An analysis and evaluation of taste.* New York: Basic Books.

Goldberg, Steven E., & Strain, Charles R. (Eds.). (1987). *Technological change and the transformation of America.* Carbondale: Southern Illinois University Press.

Gusfield, Joseph R. (1967). Tradition and modernity: Misplaced polarities in the study of social change. *American Journal of Sociology, 72,* 351-362.

Hall, Stuart (1979). Culture, media, and the ideological effect. In James Curran, Michael Gurevitch, & Janet Woollacott (Eds.), *Mass communication and society.* Beverly Hills, CA: Sage.

Hall, Stuart (1982). The rediscovery of "ideology": Return of the repressed in media studies. In Michael Gurevitch, Tony Bennett, James Curran, & Janet Woollacott (Eds.), *Culture, society and the media.* New York: Methuen.

Hall, Stuart, & Whannel, Paddy (1964). *The popular arts.* New York: Pantheon.

Haskell, Thomas L. (1977). *The emergence of professional social science: The American Social Science Association and the nineteenth-century crisis of authority.* Urbana: University of Illinois Press.

Hassan, Ihab (1986). The culture of postmodernism. In Monique Chefdor, Ricardo Quinones, & Alebert Wachtel (Eds.), *Modernism, challenges and perspectives.* Urbana: University of Illinois Press.

Innis, Harold Adams (1951). *The bias of communication.* Toronto: University of Toronto Press.

Innis, Harold Adams (1972). *Empire and communications.* Toronto: University of Toronto Press.

Jacobs, Norman (Ed.). (1961). *Culture for the millions? Mass media in modern society.* Princeton, NJ: Van Nostrand.

Jameson, Frederic (1984). Postmodernism, or the cultural logic of late capitalism. *New Left Review, 146,* 53-92.

Jarrell, Randall (1961). A sad heart at the supermarket. In Norman Jacobs (Ed.), *Culture for the millions? Mass media in modern society.* Princeton, NJ: Van Nostrand.

Jay, Martin (1973). *The dialectical imagination: A history of the Frankfurt school and the Institute of Social Research, 1923-1950.* London: Heinemann.

Jensen, Joli K. (1984). *Creating the Nashville sound: A case study in commercial music production.* Unpublished doctoral dissertation, University of Illinois.

Jensen, Joli K. (1987, November). *Writing with a machine: Typewriting and the literary marketplace at the turn of the century.* Paper presented at the annual meeting of the American Studies Association.

Jensen, Joli K. (1988). Genre and recalcitrance: Country music's move uptown. *Tracking: Popular Music Studies, 1*(1).

Klapp, Orrin (1986). *Overload and boredom: Essays on the quality of life in the information society.* Westport, CT: Greenwood.

Kowenhoven, John A. (1949). *Made in America: The arts in modern civilization.* Garden City, NY: Doubleday.

Layton, Edwin T. (Ed.). (1973). *Technology and social change in America.* New York: Harper & Row.

Lazere, Donald (Ed.). (1987). *American media and mass culture: Left perspectives.* Berkeley: University of California Press.

Lears, T. J. Jackson (1981). *No place of grace: Antimodernism and the transformation of American culture 1880-1920.* New York: Pantheon.

Lifton, Robert Jay (1968). Protean man. *Partisan Review, 35*(1).

Lippmann, Walter (1922). *Public opinion.* New York: Macmillan.

Macdonald, Dwight (1944). A theory of popular culture. *Politics, 1*(1), 20-23.

Macdonald, Dwight (1962). *Against the American grain.* New York: Random House.

Mander, Jerry (1978). *Four arguments for the elimination of television.* New York: Morrow.

Marquis, Alice Goldfarb (1986). *Hopes and ashes: The birth of modern times 1929-1939.* New York: Free Press.

Marx, Leo (1964). *The machine in the garden: Technology and the pastoral ideal in America.* New York: Oxford University Press.

Marx, Leo (1976). *The American Revolution and the American landscape.* Bicentennial Address presented at the University of Virginia, Charlottesville.

McLuhan, Marshall (1962). *The Gutenberg galaxy: The making of typographic man.* Toronto: University of Toronto Press.

McLuhan, Marshall (1964). *Understanding media: The extensions of man.* New York: New American Library.

McRobbie, Angela (1986). The Soweto dash. In Lisa Appignanensi & Geoff Bennington (Eds.), *Postmodernism: ICA Documents 4.* London: Institute of Contemporary Arts.

Merquior, J. P. (1986). The spider and the bee. In Lisa Appignanensi & Geoff Bennington (Eds.), *Postmodernism: ICA Documents 4.* London: Institute of Contemporary Arts.

Meyer, Donald (1980). *The positive thinkers: Religion as pop psychology from Mary Baker Eddy to Oral Roberts.* New York: Pantheon.

Mills, C. Wright (1956). *The power elite.* New York: Oxford University Press.

Mumford, Lewis (1926). *The golden day: A study in American experience and culture.* New York: Boni & Liveright.

Mumford, Lewis (1973). *Interpretations and forecasts: 1922-1972, studies in literature, history, biography, technics, and contemporary society.* New York: Harcourt Brace Jovanovich.

Newcomb, Horace (1974). *TV: The most popular art.* Garden City, NY: Anchor.

Newcomb, Horace (Ed.). (1987). *Television: The critical view* (4th ed.). New York: Oxford University Press.

Nisbet, Robert A. (1966). *The sociological tradition.* New York: Basic Books.

Ong, Walter J. (1982). *Orality and literacy: The technologizing of the word.* New York: Methuen.

Parker, Gail Thain (1973). *Mind cure in New England: From the Civil War to World War I.* Hanover, NH: University Press of New England.

Pearsons, Stow (1973). *The decline of American gentility.* New York: Columbia University Press.

Peterson, Theodore (1956). The social responsibility theory of the press. In Fred S. Siebert, Theodore Peterson, & Wilbur Schramm (Eds.), *Four theories of the press.* Urbana: University of Illinois Press.

Postman, Neil (1985). *Amusing ourselves to death: Public discourse in the age of show business.* New York: Viking.

Rabinow, Paul, & Sullivan, William M. (Eds.). (1979). *Interpretive social science: A reader.* Berkeley: University of California Press.

Rorty, Richard (1982). *Consequences of pragmatism: Essays 1972-1980.* Minneapolis: University of Minnesota Press.

Rorty, Richard (1989). *Contingency, irony and solidarity.* New York: Cambridge University Press.

Rosenberg, Bernard, & White, David Manning (Eds.). (1957). *Mass culture: The popular arts in America.* Glencoe, IL: Free Press.

Rosenberg, Bernard, & White, David Manning (Eds.). (1971). *Mass culture revisited.* New York: Van Nostrand Reinhold.

Rossiter, Clinton, & Lare, James (Eds.). (1963). *The essential Walter Lippmann.* New York: Random House.

Rourke, Constance (1942). *The roots of American culture and other essays.* New York: Harcourt, Brace.

Rowland, Willard D., Jr. (1983). *The politics of TV violence: Policy uses of communication research.* Beverly Hills, CA: Sage.

Schudson, Michael (1978). *Discovering the news: A social history of American newspapers.* New York: Basic Books.

Segal, Howard P. (1985). *Technological utopianism in American culture.* Chicago: University of Chicago Press.

Shils, Edward (1971). Mass society and its culture. In Bernard Rosenberg & David Manning White (Eds.), *Mass culture revisited.* New York: Van Nostrand Reinhold.

Thorburn, David (1988). Television as an aesthetic medium In James W. Carey (Ed.), *Media, myths and narratives: Television and the press.* Newbury Park, CA: Sage.

Tocqueville, Alexis de (1956). *Democracy in America* (Richard D. Heffner, ed.). New York: New American Library. (Original work published 1835)

Trine, Ralph Waldo (1897). *In tune with the infinite, or fullness of peace, power and plenty.* New York: Thomas Y. Crowell.

White, David Manning (1970). *Pop culture in America.* Chicago: Quadrangle.

Whitman, Walt (1959). Democratic vistas. In James E. Miller, Jr. (Ed.), *Complete poetry and selected prose by Walt Whitman.* Boston: Houghton Mifflin. (Original work published 1871)

Wiebe, Robert (1967). *The search for order, 1877-1920.* New York: Hill & Wang.

Williams, Frederick (1982). *The communications revolution.* Beverly Hills, CA: Sage.

Wilson, Christopher P. (1985). *The labor of words: Literary professionalism in the progressive era.* Athens: University of Georgia Press.

Winn, Marie (1977). *The plug-in drug.* New York: Viking.

Index

A Sad Heart at the Supermarket, Jarrell, 109

Accurate knowledge, protects public, 78

Actual reality, Boorstin's, 30

Administrative research, 153, 154, 155

Advent of new media, advocacy and attack/period of prediction, 95

Advertising: civilizing influence, 40; education, 148; illusion/designed to trick, 72, 173; consumer culture/refiguring beliefs, 38; ideological impact, 41; individualism paradox, 40

Aesthetic: ability, 162; community, 113; criteria/evaluation, 104, 105; experience, 114; hierarchies, 26; relationism, 113; standards, 28, 79; taste, 119; worth, 187

Against the American Grain, Macdonald, 19, 21, 25; antidemocratic implications, 21; descriptive analysis of, 20-30; influence of mass culture on high culture, 21; levels of modern culture, 21; metaphors and assumptions, 23; need for cultural classes, 25

Age of Exposition, 46

Age of Show Business, 46

Agrarian community change to industrial society, 42

Alienation, 83, 84

Alienation/progress dyad, 83-85

America beliefs and principles, 69; tainted and transfigured by progress, 175

American classics, enriching life, 108

American commentary, description of, 14

American criticism, major themes of, 156; ambivalences, 21

American critics, justification of anti-popular aesthetic evaluations, 117

American cultural mythology, effects on criticism, 123

American culture theory, themes of/mass media criticism, 118

American culture, untapped potential, 121; duality in evaluating, 118

American expectations, of transformation, 95

American heritage, 69, 70

American Imagination, The, Bode, 118

American life, lost promise, 175

American mass society theory, relation to utopian dreams, 71; fear of the public, 74

American media criticism: essentialist view of, 123; populist impulse/European heritage, 117

American "natural spirit"/European "cultivation" dichotomy, 118

American opinion, shaped by belief and conjecture, 157

American social theory, concerns, 75; public as active force, 76

American social thought, unresolved tensions, 70; liberal, individualist heritage, 69; education and mass media, 154-155; issue of connection, 71

American story of technological and intellectual progress, 62

American vernacular tradition/culture, renewal of, 119; ideal compared to media, 120

American "vigor"/European "decadence," 118

Amusement, as danger, 47

Amusing Ourselves to Death, Postman, 19; descriptive analysis of, 44-50

Anomie, 84-85

Antimodernist practices, Lear's analysis, 86

Apocalyptic vision, media, 10

Arendt, Hannah, 109, 110

Art, 185, 186, 187; commerce, distinction, 41, 170 (inherent contradictions, 42; opposition of, 167; polluted by, 172); defined, 184 (Matthew Arnold's, 108); distinct from life, 108-109, 110; ennobling, 110, 159; European forms eclipsed, 172; experience, 126; historically grounded, socially located, contingent practice, 185; information compared, 145 (distinctions between, 162); inherent worth/uplifting, 161; media, dichotomy of, 115; nonart, 34; popularized, 172; pure, 168, 170, 171; redemptive, 109,161, 170; romantic view of, 115, 116; separate sphere-effects of, 110; systems of legitimation/patronage, 186; unifying and humanizing, 171; vernacular conception of, 161

Artist's/hack's goals contrasted, 115

Artistic: community, notion of, 115; expression, 114; merit, reconceptualized, 105; strangulation, 41

Artness, 104

Arts and facts, as tradition, 73

Arts and news, to be protected, 164

Assumptions, connections of, 156

Atomized social relations, 71, 73

Audience: as barbaric, 187; bashing, 53-54; incapacitated by mass media, 54; transformed, 155; victims, 174

Authenticity, Berman's analysis, 86-87; naturalness, 86

Authority/Power dichotomy, 74-78

Authors, sanctified by Art, 170

Automatic control, vulnerable to, 151

Back to Basics movement, 146

Bad culture, appeal of, 162; moral danger from, 53

Bell, Daniel, 66, 67; summary of mass society argument, 66-67

Bellah, Robert N., et al., 72

Bias, entertainment, news, television, 126

Bode, Carl, 118

Boorstin and Ewen, comparisons, 37

Boorstin and Macdonald, comparisons, 32

Boorstin and Postman, agreements, 46

Boorstin, Daniel, 19, 57, 73, 77, 127, 133, 140, 156, 172; concern with truth, 30; fate of reality, 51; points of view, 30-37; primary influence of media is cognitive, 51; role of media in illusions, pseudo-events, 51

Boundaries, between good and evil, 159; as real, 50; blurring causes catastrophe, 172; defended, 167; lines of demarcation, 159-160; narrative key to mythic stories, 159; transgression/breakdown of, 159, 160

Boundedness, processes of, 166

Bramson, Leon, 69, 70; summary of views, 69-70

Brave New World, Huxley, 47, 92

Brown's Ideal Types, 60

Calvinism, mistrust of emotion, 169

Canons and distinctions, as anchors and bulwarks, 197

Capitalism, equated with oppression, 43

Captains of Consciousness: Advertising and the Social Roots of the Consumer Culture, Ewen, 19; descriptive analysis of, 38-44

Captains of industry as captains of consciousness, 39

Carey, James W., 56, 100, 125, 129, 137; and Kreiling, criticism of two-step flow model, 153; and Quirk, "rhetoric of the electric sublime", 94-95

Celebrities and heroes, blurred distinctions, 34

Censorship, danger of, 133

Change, evaluation of, 57, 58

Cheney, Lynne V., 106

Children, vulnerable, 149, 150; conduits of Ideology, 40; television, 150

Class/Status dichotomy, 78-80

Climate of opinion, 9, 12

Coherence, imposed on world, 128

Commentary, historical trajectory of, 102

Commerce, alienating and dehumanizing, 171; Art as separate realms, 41; corrupting/polluting force, 42, 148, 168, 170, 171; deforming Art, 41; profane, 170

Commercial system, mistrust of, 148

Commission on Freedom of the Press, 135

Common man, worthiness of, 117

Communal: correctness, 116; relationships/standards, 114; ties, 192

Communication forms: association forms/cultural participation, 193; developmental relationships, 183; electronic/oral/printing/writing, 182; historical transformations, 182; possibilities and limits/tendencies, 182

Communication technologies, failure to redeem, 193

Communication: linear transmission model/view of, 125, 127-128, 166; ritual model/view of, 125, 166; social inquiry, 138

Communities, contrasted with societies, 71

"Community of publics" contrasted with "society of masses", 77

Community/Society dichotomy, 71-74

Connections, issue of, 71

Conscious/unconscious dichotomy, 151

Conservative critique, 113

Consumer culture, panacea, 37; false community, 72

Consumers, educated to values of capitalism, 148

Consumption, as alternative to social action, 38

Contamination, notion of, 166

Context-free information, 46

Contradictory premises, made invisible, 165

Corporate values placed in home, 40

Corruption of innocence, 175

Crisis in humanistic scholarship, 104

"Crisis of authority" and loss of democratic community, 77

Critical discourse, ideal forms used to evaluate media, 178; mystical solutions offered/redemption, 178; people as corrupt or corruptible, 178

Critical elitism as amulets, 43

Criticism, basic structure, 55

Critics, magical claims, 54-55; uninfluenced by media education, 149

Critique: of corruption, mobilization of, 101; of popular culture, inherent contradictions, 27; of the critique, 18

Crowd/mob vision, 165

"Cultural" and "natural" distinctions, 37

Cultural boundaries, 29

Cultural classes, 25

Cultural conceptualization, alternatives, 178

Cultural connectedness, and media power, 183

Cultural content and egalitarian, democratic society, 79

Cultural criticism, vernacular distinctions, 167; essential flaw, 179

Cultural decline, crucial aspect of modernity, 175

Cultural dissensus, 112

Cultural forms, hierarchies, 116, 164; operation of, 187; popularity equated with lower form/unworthy, 116-117, 123; social status, 79, 112

Cultural industries, definition of, 21

Cultural levels, distinction of, 21; of material, 111; relation to taste cultures and publics, 113

Cultural mobility, 113

Cultural worth, inescapable elitism, 112

Culture cultivating an audience, 28

Darwin, Charles, 169

Davis, Robert E., popular discourse research, 95

Demise of localized cultures and creative expression, 41

Democratic art, 119, 122, 123, 124

Democratic literature, 121

Democratic society, created and maintained, 199

Democratic taste opposed to European affectations, 119

Democratic Vistas, Whitman's, 120

Demons of discourse, irrelevance, impotence, and incoherence, 46

Dewey, John, 137, 146

Diabolical irony, Boorstin's, 32

Direct Effects model, 155; *see also* Hypodermic Needle model

Disclaimers, 16-17

Discourse, definition of, 13; animating optimism, 193

Discriminatory ability, 162

Disruption and disintegration narrative, modernity as, 62

Distinctions, 197

Divine Literatus, 120, 121, 122

Douglas, Ann, 171

Douglas, Mary, 168

Dr. Jekyll and Mr. Hyde, 169

Durkheim, 67

Durkheimian and Weberian concepts, transformation of, 70

Dystopian vision of future, 92

Economic relations obscured by ideology, 43

Education, 187, 189; ambiguous role/dichotomy, 146, 147, 155; American notions of, 145-146 (social thought, 154-155); conflicting expectations/assumptions, 146, 147, 190; cultivation of sensibilities, 146; curriculum, 48,189; defined, 185; development of critical faculties, 149; historically locatable, socially grounded, value-laden, 149, 189; incompatible with corporate values, 147-148; interests and purposes served, 190; process of acculturation and socialization, 190; redemptive, 187; rethinking cultural hierarchies, 189; ritual view of, 166; social construct, 145; social need, 147; transcendence source, 149; transmission view of, 166; transmitting knowledge, 146; wisdom in foolish world, 159

Egalitarian populism, 21

Elitist viewpoints, European and American, 78-79

Emotion, enlightenment distinction of, 168; mistrust of/polluting, 168, 169; power over reason, 172

Enlightenment, natural beliefs, 119; distinction between reason and emotion, 168

Entertainment: bias of, 126; contrasted with culture, 110; natural format of experience, 47; popular genres as most worthy, 163; trivializer, 50

Entertainment media loyal to popularity, 172

Entertainment programming, evaluation of, 143; dangerous/unrealistic, 141, 142

Epistemology, print/television-based, 45-47

European, conceptualizations, reworking of, 70; sociological thought and the "crowd", 152

European mass society theory, central claims, 67; image of social disintegration, 69; in American critique, 70; nostalgic emphasis, 68

Evaluation, socially determined/consensual process, 180; consensus, complexities of, 184; cultural practice, 197; interests and purposes served, 188

Ewen, Stuart, 19, 37, 57, 72, 127, 133, 140, 148, 156, 172; assumptions, 43; Boorstin, comparisons, 37; fate of social relations, 51; points of view, 38-44; media as ideological/consumption, 51

Facts, contrasted with opinions, 139; reliability challenged, 131; separated from values, 144

Factuality, as criterion, 129

Fallacy of traditional cultures as consistent and normative, 61

Family unit as focus of Ideology of Consumption, 40

Folk Art, 22, 111; relationship between producer and audience, 113-114

Folk artists, in-tune, 115

Folk culture, 20

Folkways, 65, 66, 68, 70

Four Arguments for the Elimination of Television, Mander, 150

Frank, Waldo, 121

Frankfurt School, 67, 71, 73

Franklin, Benjamin, 146

Freedom of choice, as naive notion, 153

Freedom of press, 31, 133

Gans, Herbert, 113

Good and evil juxtaposition, mistrusted, 195

Good arts, defined, 106-107

Good stuff, defined, 53

Good taste, of the people deflected by industry/media, 121-122

Graphic Revolution: Boorstin's, 32, 34; paradox of, 34

"Great Community," Dewey's, 138

Gusfield, Joseph R., 61, 62; seven fallacies of traditional/modern polarity, 61

Habits of the Heart, Bellah et al., 72

Hall, Stuart, 99, 153

Handlin, Oscar, 114

High Culture, 21, 111; definition of, 22-23; relationship between producer and audience, 113-114

Highest characteristics, rarely shared and unequally distributed, 163

Home and business world, distinctions of, 171

Human constructions, judged by influence, 196

Humanities in America, Cheney's NEH Report, 106, 107, 108, 109, 110; summary of, 106-108

Humans, as biologically natural and cultural, 196

Huxley, Aldous, 47

Hypnosis, media/television, 151

Hypnotic images/power of television, 151, 155

Hypodermic Needle model of media effects, 152; *see also* Direct Effects model

Idea of progress, 57; evaluation standard/underlying change, 58

Ideal forms of communication contrasted with mass media, 73-74; challenged, 188

Ideal world, transcends reality, 195

Ideological context ignored, 153

Ideological influence of media content, 155

Ideological processes hidden, 153

Ideology, works by exclusion, 153-154; implicit structuring, 155

Ideology of consumption, 38, 39, 40; advertising/public relations relationship, 40; cultivator of loyalty, 39; definer of social realm/family unit as focus, 40; mystifying fundamental relationships, 41-42; securing consent of oppressed, 42

Illusions mask information, 127

Image and ideal, blurred distinctions, 34
Image: A Guide to Pseudo-Events in America, The, Boorstin, 19, 30; descriptive analysis of, 30-37
Images, pseudo-events contrasted with reality, 35-36
Implicit structuring and ideology, 155
Impotence, as low information/action ratio, 46
Individual, at the mercy of the media, 72
Individualism, related to alienation/progress, 83
Industrial Revolution, as precipitating force, 167
Inequities of corporate capitalism, 37
Information, 187, 188; affecting perception, 145; and Art compared, 145; characteristic of all culture forms, 143; commodity, 134, 136, 140; defined, 184; dispassionate form of communication, 131; distribution aids democracy, 144; epistemological assumptions, 188; ideal, 188; masked by illusions, 127; modern value, 138; neutral/value free, 132, 144; panacea, 184; propaganda, 127; redemptive, 161, 187; trusted, 140; truth in illusory world, 159; vernacular conception of, 161; worth/value of, 140, 161
Information Age, 94
Information center/bureau, Lippmann's, 137
Information model, 125; dominant critical perspective, 127; historical locatable assumptions, 129; of media, people need outside agencies, 136; research agenda, 127
Information transmission, as linear, particularistic, and mechanistic, 138; of messages, 124
Informed citizens vision, 165
Informed public contrasted with rabble, 165
Innovation, 193

Intellectual: currents, American founding beliefs, 119; weeklies, as purveyors of High Culture, 29
Interchangeable cultural forms, 34
Interpretive approach contrasted with positivist perspective, 128
Issue of representation, 126

Jarrell, Randall, 109, 110
Journalism: American social thought, 126; class distinctions, 131; education development of, 135; focus of criticism, 125; history of, 130; ideal, 136, 139, 140; information model as higher class, 131; linked to information metaphor, 129; model/moral distinctions, 131; objective-oriented threaten by entertainment-oriented, 130; professionalization of, 130, 135, 136; pseudo-events, 31; reason superior to emotion, 131; social scientific, 137
Journalism Story, telling versus information-based, 130, 131; model as lower class, 131
Journalists, information brokers, 137-138; proxies of the public, 139; sanctified by Truth, 170

Klapp, Orrin, views of progress, 84
Knowledge, necessary or valuable, 190; transmissible commodity, 144

Levels of culture, Edward Shils', 111-112; appeal to different levels of people, 112; superior, mediocre, and brutal, 112
Liberal critique, 113
Libertarian heritage, challenge to by vernacular social theory, 163
Libertarian model of news, opinion circulators, 136
Libertarian theory, 164
Libertarian theory of the press, 133
Lifton, Robert J., views of progress, 84

Lippmann, Walter, 137, 146
Logical Positivism, 138-139
Lost ability to discriminate real from sham, 31
Lowest characteristics, as widely shared, 163
Lowest Common Denominator, 114, 162, 163, 164, 184; appeal of, 162; concept not questioned, 163; rebuke to media, 163

Macdonald, Dwight, 19, 57, 73, 79, 111, 113, 156, 164, 172; compared with Boorstin, 32; fate of High Culture, 50; points of view, 20-30; primary influence of media is aesthetic, 50-51; role of media threat to Art - 50
Magical claims about media, 54-55
Man: animalistic emotions of, 169; gifted with reason, under siege, 169
Mander, Jerry, 150
Market considerations, determination of content, 172
Marx, Leo, 119, 175
Marxist, arguments, Ewen's, 43-44; critique challenged, 43-44
Mass art, as pandering, 123
Mass audience, cultivated by media values, 149
Mass communication, 182; blamed, 75; commentary on, 18; dissemination of ideal forms, 184; research, 70, 153, 154, 155
Mass Culture, 20; and mass society, 191; debate, 111 (description of, 20-21; elitism of, 117; main thrusts, 111); defined, 39
Mass democracy, questioned, 64
Mass literature, 170
Mass society, concept of, 66; "atomized" relations, 71; contrasted with traditional communities, 66; disrupting force, 66; European conception, 69; European/American critique contrasted, 70; fear of, 191; mass culture, 29, 66

Mass society theory, 65-66; American "traditional" communities, 68; Bell's criticism of, 67; Bell's summary, 66; conceptual model, 67; emergence of, 65; folk communities overwhelmed, 65-66; nostalgic emphasis of, 68; problems in American social thought, 68; shattered bonds, 67, 75; social narrative, 67
Masscult, 21, 111; and High Culture, key distinction, 23; connection with Industrial Revolution, 22; formulaic, 23; source of/transformation of Folk Art, 22
Masscult & Midcult, Macdonald, 21
Masses, as reciprocating engine, 27; untrustworthy, 79
Master Metaphor, of media, 101
Materialistic forces overwhelming spiritual impulses, 121
Media, definitions of, 19, 58; alien forms, 85; and art criticism, 103; and Third World/cultural imperialism, 154; and utopian society, 89; antithetical to High or Folk Art, 116; apocalyptic vision, 10; appeal to emotion/humanness, 163, 171; Art, resistance to, 111; as art form, 101, 105; aspect of image representation, 32; aspects of contemporary culture, 200; attitudes toward, 12, 112; blurring distinctions/boundaries, 167, 171, 172; castigated for bias, 185; catering to barbaric tendencies, 184; commercially based, 147; compared to idealized forms, 185; conduits, 110; contrasted with artistic expression, 114; corrodes what is important, 51-52; critics of, 18; cultural process, 183; deforming democratic taste, 122; destabilizing/disruptive influence, 62, 73; educational institution/tool, 101, 145, 149, 154; emblematic of modernity, 65; endowed with seductive power, 54, 160; expectations, related to political de-

mocracy, 77; extensions of mass society, 73; failure to provide information causing evil, 144; forms of response, 145; global village, 82; human-made forms of cultural significance, 179; ideological apparatuses, 42, 154; inadequate art, information, or education, 102; inauthentic other, 87; incapacitates audience, 54; information conduits/source, 101, 125, 139, 142, 143; listened to, 199; mediator between politicians and people, 78; mirrors or windows of reality, 128; mixing of art with commerce, 171; modernity, 64, 85; new form of connectedness, 183; part of social and cultural process, 179; polluter, 50, 88, 174; power to transform, 180; powerful to be blamed, 165; primary vehicles in critique of modernity, 62; provider of specious identities and aspirations, 148; purveyors of Mass Culture, 29; redeemer, 81; safeguard of democracy, 78; scapegoat, 58, 65, 76, 124, 175-176, 185, 191, 192; self-interested ways, 77; serpent or sirens, 160, 173, 175; site for collective conversation, 201; social responsibility, 142, 164; status battleground, 79; technology, 32, 97; threat to dispassionate communication, 172; totalizing influence, 181; transcendence offered by education/information, 81; transformer, 52-55, 76; "uses and gratifications" of, 152, 153; victims of, 10; villain and potential hero, 58; villain, critical win-win situation, 65; Whitman's criticism of, 120; window on the world, 126; world picture, 144

Media accounts substituted for reality, 77

Media attacks, vehemence of, 75; explained, 81

Media audience, vulnerable, 73; instinctual desire for "bad stuff", 53

Media blamed, 54, 64, 75-76, 124, 164, 173, 181, 194; exoneration, 195; for corruption and deflection, 21, 88, 89, 116, 160, 174; for inadequacies, 64; inappropriately for ills, 201; prevents recognition of contemporary conditions, 200-201

Media choice, criticized, 153

Media commentary, definition of, 13; as lens, 14; political aspect, 16

Media conceptualization alternatives, 178

Media content, as ideology, 43, 155; blurs distinctions, 173-174; designed to be seductive, 173

Media criticism, 18; as critique of modern life, 64, 192; beliefs, 57; blames unnatural intervention, 182; disrespectful attitude of, 181-182; intersection with social criticism, 15; mythic basis/narrative structure of, 55

Media critics, as protector, 197; define "good stuff", 53; deplores tastes and choices made, 181; waiting for salvation, 194

Media critique, 20th-century tensions, 70; and automatically redemptive culture, 186; conundrum about public taste, 53

Media discourse, 98; American connections, 14; as social narrative and myth of seduction, 160; body of literature, 18; contradictions of, 157; definition of, 13; logic of, 17; reconceptualization, 198

Media effects, on individuals/society, 174; lack of research effect, 17

Media influence, 55; blamed/corrupting force, 101-102; claims of, 97, 101; fear of, 191; in ideological structure of values, 153; mitigated by social patterns, 152

Media messages, as "two-step flow", 152, 153; prestructured, 154

Media metaphors, 17, 101

Media of communication, as dominant influence, 45

"Media of the future", as positive force, 89

Media opposition to Art parallel modernity opposition to tradition, 116

Media participation, as trusting and passive, 173

Media power, 75, 78; as cultural conversation/connectedness, 182, 183; categories of, 173; destructive/corrupt, 54, 181; psychological/cultural, 181

Media reform, administrative solution, 88

Media study, curriculum justification, 104

Media technology, as hypnotic, 173

Media-based unreality as Ideological, 37

Media-in-society, conceptualizations of, 12; climate of opinion, 9

Media-induced decline, in American life, 174

Media/modernity critique, natural good deformed/utopian potential, 195

Media/modernity discourse, 191; absolves from responsibilities/active engagement, 194, 195; as American form, 194; as convincing, 161; evaluative distinctions, 198

Media/modernity narrative, boundaries, 196

Media/modernity story, simplistic, elitist, and naive, 177; makeshift quality, 177; places blame outside ourselves, 177; risk of, 191

Media/modernity, social narrative, 198; avoidance of paradoxes and contradictions, 191; lack of neutral evaluative ground, 179; participation and understanding, 199; placing of

blame, 191; reconceptualization, 191; story of pollution, 197

Medium, modern, mass-mediated culture, 109; corrupting, 109; transformer, 110

Men, materialistic/rational, 169, 171

Messages, linear model of, 125

Metaphor: art, 123, 138, 140, 145, 154, 159, 164, 166; breakdown and disintegration, 66; chewing gum, 35; cultivation, 25, 79-80; education, 138, 145, 154, 159, 164, 166; food, 33, 35; information, 124, 126, 138, 139, 144, 145, 154, 159, 164, 166; ingestion, 25; plague, 36; tourism, 33; vision, 30

Metropolis, Lang's, 92

Midcult, 21, 111; corruption of High Culture, 24-25; danger of, 24

Mills, C. Wright, 76, 148

Misinformed public, vulnerable to totalitarianism, 78

Mistrust of commercialization, 42

Mob, as irrational public, 74

Mobilization of critique of corruption, 101

Modern, contemporary culture, 59; conceptualized as conflicting with traditional, 61

Modern Age, as secular, 80; originating moments/technological innovations of, 60

Modern and premodern times, distinction between, 59

Modern condition, 192

Modern influence on traditional, 61

Modern life discussions, contradiction, 192

Modern society, 192

Modern Times, Chaplin's, 92

Modern values, 192

Modernity, 57; and premodernity, conceptual stability, 60; betrayal of promise, 59; blamed, 75; complaints of abundance, 200; conceptual fuzziness of, 60; conceptualized destructive outside influence, 61; corrupting innocence, 62; criticism of, 57; cultural decline, 175; disintegration of community, 66; Enlightenment legacy, 198; evaluated in relation to assumptions, 179; history transformed into argument, 200; influence on quality of individual experience, 84; international evaluation of, 60; intractable issues of, 64; liberating force, 62; loss of former grace/path to future grace, 58; loss of spiritual welfare, 175; media criticism intersects social criticism, 15; multifaceted condition, 200; multiplies interpretive worlds, 199; offering weak and evanescent connections, 72; overall effect of, 72; positive force, 70; problem of receding origins, 59; progressive achievement, 89; realized potential, 91; recognizing/questioning cultural web, 198; shares narrative with media, 62; social/cultural/"age" change, 59; socially constructed story, 179; tensions of, 192; unnatural, 85; use of seduction and betrayal myth, 62, 160; variety of, 200; weakens tradition, 62

Modernity critique, 20th Century tensions, 70; beliefs of, 192; luxurious intellectual despair, 195

Modernity discourse, 57; reproduction of rural/urban tension, 62

Modernity narrative, decadent finale or desirable prelude, 89

Moral danger in "bad stuff", 53

Moral value in "good stuff", 53

Moral and aesthetic forms, dissolving, 35

Mumford, Lewis, 100

Myth: of Frankenstein, 169; of media influence, boundaries and consequences of transgression, 160; of progress, 57; of Seduction, 159, 160, 166, 172; of the artist, 115; of the Garden of Eden, 55, 159, 160, 174; of the

Lorelei, 55, 159, 160, 174; romantic nature of art, 115

Mythic basis of criticism, 55

Mythic stories, boundaries as narrative key, 159

Narrative: of loss, 193; of Seduction, 162; structure of media criticism, 55

"National self-hypnosis", Boorstin's, 31

"Natural" and "cultivated" tensions, 117

"Natural" and "cultural" distinctions, 37

Natural aristocracy, emergence of, 74

Natural/artificial, as illusory distinctions, 196

Nature/culture tension, 37

Neurasthenia, 84

Neurophysiological consequences, of television, 150-151

New technologies, as redemptive, 94; same dreams and nightmares, 97

Newcomb, Horace, 157

News, as information, 139; as neutral, 165; bias of, 126; ideal, 188; popular genres as most worthy, 163

News Media, fundamental beliefs about, 125; concern about, 76; Dewey's view, 76; evaluation of, 140-141; Lippmann's view, 76; Mills' view and critique, 76-77; objective requirement, 126

News Process as public information process, 125

Newspapers, 134

Newspeople, define new role as middleman, 135

Nisbet, Robert, 71

Objective information, epistemological impossibility/talisman, 188

Objectivity, contrasted with subjectivity, 132; mistrust of, 131; news value, 129; "peculiar demand" of news, 130; quest for certainty, 132; recent development, 132; talisman, 132

Open marketplace of ideas, 133

Opinion, as forced-choice situation, 153

Order/chaos, belief, 167; demarcations of, 168

Organizations, extending undemocratic power, 149

Orwell, George, 48; *1984*, 48, 92

Outside influence, as central theme, 61

Participatory democracy, notion of, 181

Passive stance, naturalizes social change, 193

Past as prelude, modernity as improving, 90

Past culture forms unrealistic, 143

Patriarchy reconstituted in capitalism, 40

People: as helpless victims, 122; as good and worthy, 164; as naturally crude and animalistic, 163, 164; as unevenly endowed, 164; insensitive to Art, 122; hierarchically organized, as un-American, 164

People's choices, a priori corrupt, 181

Perceptions as fictions, 36

Pessimistic outlook, as veneer, 93

Peterson, Theodore, 134

Political campaigns, as "feel good" images, 48

"Political" scholarship reprimanded, 107

Politics of authenticity, 87

Pollution, theme, 174; beliefs/danger in society, 168

Popular Culture and High Culture, Herbert Gans', 113

Popularity, of "unworthy" cultural forms, 123; damned, 114

Popularization, as vulgarizing, 28; of Art, 34

Positive modernity, exciting present and desirable future, 90

Positive portrayals, 143

Positivist perspective contrasted with interpretive approach, 128

Postman, Neil, 19, 57, 77, 107, 126, 140, 142, 156, 172; absence of notion of art or literature, 49-50; as dystopian critic, 93; concentration on content, 49; corrosion by technology, 44; dichotomy of, 50; fate of reason, logic, and coherence, 51; ignoring complicated issues of how communication works, 49; lack of explanation, 49; points of view, 44-50; presuppositions, 48-49; public discourse and media/television, 51

Postman and Boorstin, agreements, 46

Postmodern, 59

Poststructuralist theory, 103-104

Power, increasingly centralized, 149; ascribed to media, 54

Power Elite, The, Mills's, 148

Premodern, 59

Present conditions, relationship to past and future, 90

Press, role of, 134; act in interest of public, 135; as opinion purveyor transformed into information conduit, 133; code of ethics, 135; criticism of, 134-135; libertarian theory of, 133; social responsibility model, 135; theories of, 132-133

Pretelegraphic Eden, 48-49

Print, 49

Print-based: epistemology, as serious and rational, 45-46; society transformed to television-based society, 45

Producer-audience relationship, 114

Profit, determines creative expression, 172

Progress, defined/price of, 83; as overstimulation and fragmentation, 84; compared to modernity, 84

Propaganda, power of, 152; for status quo, 154

"Pseudo-context", telegraphy and photography as, 46

Pseudo-events, 30; and extravagant expectations, 35-36; anthropological interpretation, 36; as contemporary reality/knowledge of "the world", 31; blamed for, 32; dominance of, 32-33; images as, 35; substituted for reality, 127

Psychologically oriented research, 152

Public: actions deemed inappropriate, 76; consciousness, 28; misplaced faith in, 75; opinion formed by mass media, 77; poisoned by media, 122; policy, determination of, 187; purposes, complexities of ascertaining, 186; taste, as conundrum, 53; worth attacked, 64

Public and Its Problems, The, Dewey, 137

Public Opinion, Lippmann, 137

Purity rituals, 168

Quality of material, 80

Reader's obligations, 15-16

Reading, fate of, 107

Real world assumption, 127-128

Reality, portrayal of, 125, 141-142; danger of loss, 140

Reality criteria impossible to meet, 143

Reason, Enlightenment distinction of, 168; as human trait/transform animal instincts, 169; as order counteracting chaos, 170; as pure, 168, 169; as superego, 169; controls emotion/distinguishes man, 169; liberating/redemptive powers of, 168, 170; refigured, 169; reliability challenged, 131

Reason/emotion distinction strengthened, 169

Redemption, aspects of life, 80; possibility of, 62; via cultural purity, 183-184

Rediscovery of America, The, Frank, 121

Reflex arcs, 169

Reform advocated by media criticism, 44

Relativistic moral universe, fears of, 197

Religion, as entertainment, 48

Ritual model/transmission model, contrasted, 128-129; epistemological division, 129

Ritual view of communication, 155

Ritualistic behaviors and transgressions, 168

Rowland, Willard D, Jr., 99

Rural/urban duality, 62

Sacred/secular dichotomy, 80-82

Salvation, dependent on boundaries, 197

Sanctification of spheres, 80

Schudson, Michael, 129, 130, 131, 132, 134

Scientific findings, no reliable tradition, 157

Seduction, narrative of, 162

Segal, Howard, 96

Self-education, notion of, 146

Sentimental Lie, The, Douglas', 93

Separation from artistic engagement and emotional response, 50

Separatist solution, discussion of, 26

Shils, Edward, 111, 112, 163

Simmel, 67

Small town contrasted with metropolitan existence, 62-63

Social authority replaced by commercial authority, 40

Social change, comes from participatory, pluralistic conversation, 180

Social conflict, addressed, 186

Social criticism, vernacular distinctions, 167

Social Darwinism, 167, 169

Social goals, addressed, 186

Social Narrative, 13-14; alternatives, 178; analysis and evaluation possible, 178; as ideology/negotiated truces, 68; conglomeration of, 179; definition of, 67; impossible to prove or disprove, 178; logic of, 174; shape social choice, policy, and reforms, 177

Social responsibility and mass media/television, 142

Social responsibility theory, public vulnerability, 136

Social responsibility theory of press, 135, 139, 164

Social transformation and social conversation, 199

Society and Culture, Hannah Arendt's, 109-110

Society conceptualization alternatives, 178

Society, primitive contrasted with modern, 168

Society/mass media as isolating force, 74

"Spectacle of change", Ewen's, 38

Standards: communal set of, 114; Macdonald's notion, 23-24; of evaluation, 23-24, 79

Status quo, interests and purposes served, 189

Status, issue of, 79

Stereotyping, 126, 141

Story of America, story of modernity/despoiled Garden, 175

Students, educated to democratic citizenship, 148

Subjectivity, 132, 144

Substance and shadow, lack of discrimination, 35

"Synthetic novelty", Boorstin's, 30

Taste cultures/publics, 113

Technological boosterism, naivete of, 183

Technological transformation, both natural and human-made, 97

Technological utopia, demonic undercurrents, 92

Technology, connected to cultural and social purposes, 193, 194; American faith in, 82; American utopian thought, 96; antithetical to human values, 92; as transformer/redeemer/cure-all, 96; embodying progress, 96; salvation by dangerously naive, 194

Telegraph, 46

Telegraphy and photography as "pseudo-context", 46

Television: and children, 150; and social responsibility, 142; as command center, 47; as debased literature, 107; as passive activity, 150; as trivializing transformer, 44; belief it accurately reflects world, 142; bias of, 48, 126; demand for irrationality, 49; distorting reality, 141; hypnotic images/power of, 150, 151, 155; neurophysiological consequences of, 150-151; positive elements, 107

Television-based epistemology, 44-47

Television news, as entertainment, 47-48

Temptation, vulnerability to, 163

Theory of Popular Culture, A, Macdonald's, 25

"Thicket of unreality", Boorstin's, 33, 37

Tocqueville's commentary, 108

Tönnies, 67

Tradition, as legitimating principle, 62

Traditional and modern defined as mutually exclusive, 62

Traditional communities, 66, 68

Traditional society contrasted with modern society, 60-61

Traditional values, as truths and superstitions, 64

Transgression, theme, 174

Transmission model, of communication, 155; research traditions, 129

Transmission model/ritual model, contrasted, 128-129; epistemological division, 129

Two-culture "compromise", Macdonald's, 27

"Two-step flow", of media messages, 152, 153; criticism of, 153

Underlying structure of criticism as mythic, 55

"Unit ideas", Nisbet's, 71
Unresolved contradictions in American social thought, 64
Uses and gratifications of media, 152, 153

Values, separated from facts, 144; dependent on self-interested assumptions, 187; vernacular refigured, 167
Vernacular beliefs, refiguration of, 167
Vernacular cognitive theory, 162
Vernacular social theory, challenge to libertarian heritage, 163
Viewer, as passive and vulnerable, 151-152
Virtue, ambivalence of, 118
Vision of past/present, 192

Vision, egalitarian, plural American democracy, 199

Whitman, Walt, 120, 121, 122
Window of opportunity, for democracy subverted, 42
Winn, Marie, 150
Women, as irrational/spiritual, 169, 171
Workaholism, 84
World's fairs, 90-91, 93
"World of Tomorrow", 90-91
World imposed coherence on/symbolic apprehension of, 128
Worth, how ascribed, 186
Writers, commercially successful as profane, 170

About the Author

Joli Jensen is an Assistant Professor in the Radio-Television-Film Department at the University of Texas—Austin. She received her Ph.D. from the Institute of Communications Research at the University of Illinois in 1984, and taught for two years in the Department of Rhetoric and Communication Studies at the University of Virginia. She teaches courses in media in American society, media and cultural processes, communication in American social thought, qualitative research methods, and cultural studies. Her published research includes articles on commercial culture production, country music, the history of the typewriter, and fans and fandom.